OPPOSING
VIEWPOINTS®
SERIES

Iran

Other Books of Related Interest:

Opposing Viewpoints Series

Pakistan

At Issue Series

Women in Islam

Current Controversies Series

Afghanistan

"Congress shall make no law . . . abridging the freedom of speech, or of the press."

First Amendment to the U.S. Constitution

The basic foundation of our democracy is the First Amendment guarantee of freedom of expression. The Opposing Viewpoints Series is dedicated to the concept of this basic freedom and the idea that it is more important to practice it than to enshrine it.

Iran

David Haugen and Susan Musser, Book Editors

GREENHAVEN PRESS
A part of Gale, Cengage Learning

GALE
CENGAGE Learning

Detroit • New York • San Francisco • New Haven, Conn • Waterville, Maine • London

Christine Nasso, *Publisher*
Elizabeth Des Chenes, *Managing Editor*

© 2011 Greenhaven Press, a part of Gale, Cengage Learning.

Gale and Greenhaven Press are registered trademarks used herein under license.

For more information, contact:
Greenhaven Press
27500 Drake Rd.
Farmington Hills, MI 48331-3535
Or you can visit our Internet site at gale.cengage.com

For product information and technology assistance, contact us at

Gale Customer Support, 1-800-877-4253
For permission to use material from this text or product, submit all requests online at
www.cengage.com/permissions

Further permissions questions can be emailed to permissionrequest@cengage.com

Articles in Greenhaven Press anthologies are often edited for length to meet page require-ments. In addition, original titles of these works are changed to clearly present the main thesis and to explicitly indicate the author's opinion. Every effort is made to ensure that Greenhaven Press accurately reflects the original intent of the authors. Every effort has been made to trace the owners of copyrighted material.

Cover Image copyright © Javarman/Dreamstime.com.

LIBRARY OF CONGRESS CATALOGING-IN-PUBLICATION DATA

Iran / David Haugen and Susan Musser, book editors.
p. cm. -- (Opposing viewpoints)
Includes bibliographical references and index.
ISBN 978-0-7377-4972-4 (hardcover) -- ISBN 978-0-7377-4973-1 (pbk.)
1. United States--Foreign relations--Iran. 2. Iran--Foreign relations--United States. 3. Iran--Politics and government--1997- 4. Iran--Economic conditions--1997- I. Haugen, David M., 1969- II. Musser, Susan.
JZ1480.A57I7 2010
955.06--dc22
2010018203

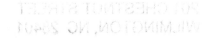

Printed in the United States of America
1 2 3 4 5 6 7 14 13 12 11 10

Contents

Chapter 3: What Was the Impact of the 2009 Iranian Presidential Election?

Chapter 4: What Are the Current Problems in Iran?

Why Consider Opposing Viewpoints?

> *"The only way in which a human being can make some approach to knowing the whole of a subject is by hearing what can be said about it by persons of every variety of opinion and studying all modes in which it can be looked at by every character of mind. No wise man ever acquired his wisdom in any mode but this."*
>
> *John Stuart Mill*

In our media-intensive culture it is not difficult to find differing opinions. Thousands of newspapers and magazines and dozens of radio and television talk shows resound with differing points of view. The difficulty lies in deciding which opinion to agree with and which "experts" seem the most credible. The more inundated we become with differing opinions and claims, the more essential it is to hone critical reading and thinking skills to evaluate these ideas. Opposing Viewpoints books address this problem directly by presenting stimulating debates that can be used to enhance and teach these skills. The varied opinions contained in each book examine many different aspects of a single issue. While examining these conveniently edited opposing views, readers can develop critical thinking skills such as the ability to compare and contrast authors' credibility, facts, argumentation styles, use of persuasive techniques, and other stylistic tools. In short, the Opposing Viewpoints Series is an ideal way to attain the higher-level thinking and reading skills so essential in a culture of diverse and contradictory opinions.

In addition to providing a tool for critical thinking, Opposing Viewpoints books challenge readers to question their own strongly held opinions and assumptions. Most people form their opinions on the basis of upbringing, peer pressure, and personal, cultural, or professional bias. By reading carefully balanced opposing views, readers must directly confront new ideas as well as the opinions of those with whom they disagree. This is not to simplistically argue that everyone who reads opposing views will—or should—change his or her opinion. Instead, the series enhances readers' understanding of their own views by encouraging confrontation with opposing ideas. Careful examination of others' views can lead to the readers' understanding of the logical inconsistencies in their own opinions, perspective on why they hold an opinion, and the consideration of the possibility that their opinion requires further evaluation.

Evaluating Other Opinions

To ensure that this type of examination occurs, Opposing Viewpoints books present all types of opinions. Prominent spokespeople on different sides of each issue as well as well-known professionals from many disciplines challenge the reader. An additional goal of the series is to provide a forum for other, less known, or even unpopular viewpoints. The opinion of an ordinary person who has had to make the decision to cut off life support from a terminally ill relative, for example, may be just as valuable and provide just as much insight as a medical ethicist's professional opinion. The editors have two additional purposes in including these less known views. One, the editors encourage readers to respect others' opinions—even when not enhanced by professional credibility. It is only by reading or listening to and objectively evaluating others' ideas that one can determine whether they are worthy of consideration. Two, the inclusion of such viewpoints encourages the important critical thinking skill of objectively evaluating an author's credentials and bias. This evaluation will illuminate an author's reasons for taking a particular stance on an issue and will aid in readers' evaluation of the author's ideas.

It is our hope that these books will give readers a deeper understanding of the issues debated and an appreciation of the complexity of even seemingly simple issues when good and honest people disagree. This awareness is particularly important in a democratic society such as ours in which people enter into public debate to determine the common good. Those with whom one disagrees should not be regarded as enemies but rather as people whose views deserve careful examination and may shed light on one's own.

Thomas Jefferson once said that "difference of opinion leads to inquiry, and inquiry to truth." Jefferson, a broadly educated man, argued that "if a nation expects to be ignorant and free . . . it expects what never was and never will be." As individuals and as a nation, it is imperative that we consider the opinions of others and examine them with skill and discernment. The Opposing Viewpoints Series is intended to help readers achieve this goal.

David L. Bender and Bruno Leone,
Founders

Introduction

> "Looking at the high level of popular mobilization and discontent, it will be very difficult to forever crush the opposition and go back to the way things were. There is now an opposition leadership that is willing to stand up to authority in Iran, not be cowed and force a debate over the status quo."
>
> —Nader Hashemi
> (author of Islam, Secularism and Liberal Democracy: Toward a Democratic Theory for Muslim Societies), Time, July 1, 2009.

On June 13, 2009, the day after the Iranian government announced that the incumbent conservative president, Mahmoud Ahmadinejad, had won a second term in office, millions of protesters took to the streets of the capital, Tehran, and other Iranian cities, claiming the presidential election was rigged. Most of the demonstrators were supporters of independent candidate Mir Hossein Mousavi, a moderate who promised to reform unjust laws and expand civil rights. Mousavi's backers adopted the color green as a symbol of their loyalty, and as the number of his supporters grew, foreign news agents dubbed the swelling opposition movement "the Green Revolution." Observers both inside and outside Iran recognized that the Green Revolution, composed mainly of young, educated Iranians, threatened the stability of the clerical regime that runs the nation. As Sam Sedaei, an international affairs contributor for *The Huffington Post* Web site, reported on June 10, 2009, Mousavi's supporters were not merely expressing a desire for reform, they were "rebelling against the fundamental theocratic structure of the Iranian political system, and the main pillars of Islamic Republic itself."

When the Green Revolution supporters flooded the streets of Tehran after the election, some held peaceful demonstrations while others took out their aggressions violently, burning tires and attacking riot police who turned out to control the crowds. During the following two days, hundreds of thousands of protesters continued to congregate in Tehran's city center. Iran's supreme leader, the Ayatollah Ali Khamenei, urged the people to accept Ahmadinejad's victory and disperse, but the masses responded with cries of "Death to the dictator." Using batons and pepper spray, the police cracked down on the demonstrators, and their aggressive efforts were abetted by gun-toting paramilitary forces supporting the president. In the melee that culminated on June 15, several people were killed; Iran state radio reported 7 dead, while other sources estimated a much higher death toll. Video images and phone transmissions brought the carnage to the outside world. The Iranian government shut down Internet and cell phone networks but could not stem the flow of news footage leaking from inside the country. A June 16 *Washington Times* editorial stated that "well-developed Twitter lists showed a constant stream of situation updates and links to photos and videos, all of which painted a portrait of the developing turmoil. Digital photos and videos proliferated and were picked up and reported in countless external sources safe from the regime's Net crackdown."

Despite the free-flowing journalism, the beatings and killings, the tightening control over media outlets, the official ban on demonstrations, and the rounding up of more than 100 opposition members took their toll on the Green Revolution. The throngs of protesters thinned after June 17, and foreign reporters acknowledged that the hoped-for overthrow of the clerical regime was not to be. Writing for *The Huffington Post* on June 17, Ali Akbar Dareini and Brian Murphy wrote, "Chances for a full-scale collapse are considered very remote. The ruling clerics still have deep public support and are defended by Iran's strongest forces, the Revolutionary Guard and a vast network of militias around the country." Only a week after the June 12 protests, the Ayatollah Khamenei assured the international community that the confrontations did not signal a rift in the Iranian system. The supreme leader called for an investigation into the election and a partial recount of the ballots, but the official independent monitoring committee found no irregularities. Many protesters wondered if their actions had been in vain, yet the crowds of black-clad mourners who peaceably assembled day after day to show respect for those killed in the demonstrations heartened the discouraged. One Iranian engineer told reporters from the *Telegraph*, a British newspaper that published his story on June 20, "Every morning I watch the news and become depressed thinking there is no chance for change. Then every afternoon I come back and see how many we are and I regain my hope and faith. I will come tomorrow and the day after and every day until they reverse this travesty."

On July 9, the protests suddenly resumed. Mousavi supporters again came out into the open even though the governor of Tehran vowed to crush any further demonstrations. Lines of police officers were on hand to carry out the governor's mandate. On that day, Nasser Karimi reported to the Associated Press, "In some places, police struck hard. Security forces chased after protesters, beating them with clubs on Valiasr Street, Tehran's biggest north-south avenue." According to journalists, the number of protesters was far smaller than it had been just a few weeks previously, perhaps totaling a few thousand. Although onlookers shouted encouragement, the show of resistance evaporated by nighttime. The government clearly was prepared this time and cut cell phone networks almost immediately to discourage protesters from coordinating their efforts. The July 9 *New York Times* quoted one Tehran resident as saying, "Protesters challenging the re-election of President Mahmoud Ahmadinejad seem to be running out of options, especially the ability to mobilize in large numbers on the streets as they did immediately after the election." This citizen noted, however, that residents in Tehran maintain one network of communication that the government could not stop—neighbors discussing events and spreading news across rooftops.

In August, Ayatollah Khamenei endorsed Ahmadinejad's presidential victory, and the incumbent resumed his office. The government also began prosecuting some of the protesters it had caught during the previous months. Crowds gathered outside the courts in Tehran, but police easily dispersed marchers who once more chanted "Death to the dictator." The following month, Mir Hossein Mousavi called on his supporters to rally against the government, but those who assembled in downtown Tehran were driven off by tear gas fired by police units. Again foreign journalists kept the vigil, and some noted that pro-government crowds were often dwarfing the protesters who turned out. The *New York Times* reported that police units refrained from punitive measures—perhaps recognizing that government supporters were keeping demonstrators in check.

Although it seemed as though the opposition was in retreat, tens of thousands of green-clad Mousavi supporters filled Tehran streets (and the streets of several other cities) on November 4, a state holiday that commemorates the takeover of the U.S. embassy in 1979, when Islamic student militants held 53 American citizens hostage in an act of revenge for U.S. support of the shah's regime. This time they clashed with armed government supporters celebrating the holiday. Security forces also were on hand and used tear gas to disrupt the violence that ensued. Several people were hospitalized, and police arrested more than 100 demonstrators. The renewed show of resistance emphasized that the opposition was not defeated. James Spencer, a Middle East expert, told the *Global-Post* Web site on November 4, "I have been amazed by the steadfastness of the protesters and their bravery." "The regime is weak, they've been unable to stop the protests using the current level of force," Spencer continued, stating that if Tehran chose to respond with military force, the soldiery might refuse to take up arms against their own people, sapping the regime of its strength.

The ongoing demonstrations—which continued in December 2009—have captured the attention of the world. While the Green Revolution does not seem to be gaining strength, its persistence suggests that modern Iran has reached a watershed moment. The chants of "Death to the dictator" reveal that the Iranian regime has lost much of its legitimacy in the eyes of the young. Although the government has retained support from poorer, less-educated Iranians who—as several commentators assert—have come to rely on government handouts, the mass of well-educated students and entrepreneurs are calling for change. One Iranian journalist, quoted in the *Los Angeles Times* on December 8, stated, "The way ahead is long. But the goal [of regime change] is achievable." Such optimism implies that the theocratic rulers that have held power in Iran for thirty years may lose their grip in the near future, as those who feel that their June votes went unheeded now clamor for true democracy. However, the Green Movement faces stiff opposition that has a lot to lose if the grip fails. Mansoor Moaddel, a professor of sociology at Eastern Michigan University, even claims that the supposedly rigged elections were an attempt by the clerical regime to dispense with representative government to impose on Iran a pure theocracy based on Islamic law. In a June 29, 2009, editorial for *Informed Consent* Web site, Moaddel expresses his fears that unless the protests continue, the last vestiges of democracy will simply disappear in Iran, and the world will acquire another extremist government—such as the Taliban in Afghanistan—bent on spreading radical Islam and attaining weapons of mass destruction.

With all eyes watching the outcome of the uprising, there is no shortage of commentary and analysis of this historic moment in Iranian history. In *Opposing Viewpoints: Iran*, several experts dissect and debate the ramifications of this struggle on the Iranian people and the international community at large. In a chapter titled "What Was the Impact of the 2009 Iranian Presidential Election?" these analysts emphasize the significance of the division now manifesting in the street clashes that have erupted throughout Iran's major cities. In other chapters—"Is Iran a Threat to the United States and Its Allies?" "How Should U.S. Foreign Policy Address Iran?" and "What Are the Current Problems in Iran?"—other commentators examine the problems that have helped foment dissent in Iran and discuss the manner in which the U.S. government should respond to the crisis. The authors included in this volume recognize that the Iran that roils in turmoil today is not the same Iran that ousted the oppressive shah in 1979, nor perhaps even the same Iran that President George W. Bush relegated to the anti-American "Axis of Evil" in 2002. These critics and observers see modern Iran at a crossroads where the population must make hard choices concerning nuclear technology, international relations, economic sustainability, and democracy. The future of Iran is written in these choices.

OPPOSING
VIEWPOINTS®
SERIES

CHAPTER 1

Is Iran a Threat to the United States and Its Allies?

Chapter Preface

Iran, which sits atop roughly 10 percent of the world's proven oil reserves and is perched along the Persian Gulf, could easily strangle 20 percent of the Middle East oil supplies that pass through that vital shipping lane. In addition, if provoked, Iran could use its strategic position in the Middle East to strike out against its oil-rich neighbors, such as Saudi Arabia, Iraq, or Kuwait, and disrupt petroleum markets around the world. U.S. analysts fear that Iran's capability of impeding oil production and driving up prices is one of the ways in which it can threaten both American and global security.

In 2005, a newspaper in the United Arab Emirates quoted Iranian President Mahmoud Ahmadinejad as saying that he might curb his country's oil production if the United Nations Security Council approved sanctions against Iran to derail its nuclear program. Although Iran's capital, Tehran, issued a statement declaring the quote to be untrue, many observers in the United States and abroad are concerned about Iran's ability to cavalierly cut oil supplies to compel the world to accede to its demands. A nearly identical threat by the Iranian oil minister in 2009 prompted similar concern; again, however, Tehran denied that the official made any such assertion.

Some U.S. experts believe that any confrontation between America and Iran would be devastating to oil prices. Christopher Ruppel, an energy analyst at Execution LLC, a brokerage and investment research company, was quoted in a July 10, 2008, CNN report stating that if the United States ever invaded Iran—which Ruppel believed was growing more likely—then "right away prices would go above $200 a barrel." Leo Drollas, deputy director and chief economist of the Center for Global Energy Studies in London, said in a July 7, 2009, *Time* magazine article that "the market will go berserk" if war came to Iran. Others, however, remain unconvinced of Iran's power.

Max Schulz, a senior fellow at the Manhattan Institute, wrote in a September 19, 2006, article for the *National Review On-line* that Iran's oil threat is quite limited. Schulz argued that while the Iranian leadership might try to stem the oil flow, the outcome would be far from disastrous. He predicted gas prices would spike at $5 to $6 per gallon, but U.S. oil reserves would take up the slack. Furthermore, Schulz claimed that the U.S. economy is strong enough to rebound from high gas prices, making Iran's threat less menacing. "Though they might cause some pain," Schulz reassured readers, "they wouldn't cripple our economy." In fact, Schulz asserted that if Tehran chose to turn off its country's oil taps, it would hurt Iran more than it would hurt the rest of the world; therefore, Schulz believed the Iranian government would not likely make good on its threat. In a more recent June 16, 2009, editorial for the San Francisco *Examiner*, Schulz maintained that tapping America's oil reserves is still the best means of easing reliance on foreign oil.

Shutting off its oil supply or disrupting regional oil production is just one of the potential threats that Iran poses to U.S. interests and world markets. Of greater concern are Iran's support of terror and its nascent nuclear program, which several leaders around the world believe are active and ongoing forms of intimidation. In the chapter that follows, U.S. experts and pundits offer their views on how serious these more pressing concerns are. Some insist that Iran's aggressive activities must be nipped quickly before it is too late to counter their potency; others maintain that no matter how strong Iran gets, it will be deterred from using its power by certain retaliation from the United States and the international community.

| "The inescapable fact is that the United States just cannot take the risk of nuclear missiles in the hands of a clerical regime that preaches genocide."

A Nuclear Iran Is a Threat to the United States and Its Allies

Mortimer Zuckerman

The acquisition of a nuclear weapon by the Iranian government has been of central concern to the United States and its allies since the Iranian Revolution of 1979 installed a theocratic government that is unfriendly to the West. While the United States helped the country begin its peaceful nuclear power program under the Shah's leadership in the 1950s, many now worry that the pursuit of nuclear power in Iran signals the government's desire to develop a nuclear weapon. Mortimer Zuckerman argues in the following viewpoint that, should Iran attain the technology necessary to construct nuclear weapons, the United States, its allies, and world security will be at risk. Zuckerman points to Iran's fundamentalist, secretive, and hostile behavior as evidence of a regime unfit to possess nuclear weapons capabilities. Zucker-

man is the editor-in-chief of the magazine *U.S. News & World
Report and he is a regular political commentator on the cable
news channel MSNBC.*

As you read, consider the following questions:

1. According to Zuckerman, how would the behavior of an
   Iran with nuclear weapons capabilities change and
   present a greater threat to the world?

2. As stated by Zuckerman, what makes a nuclear Iran a
   unique threat?

3. In the author's view, how have the U.S. presidential
   administrations' diplomatic advances toward the Iranian
   government since 1979 been received?

I ran is making fools of everyone. Even as it lies about how
close it is to acquiring nuclear missiles, it continues to menace the political order throughout the Middle East, pressing
on with rocketry and rearming Hamas and Hezbollah. And
that mischief is nothing compared to what it will do if it is allowed to become a nuclear power.

Nuclear Iran will be a threat to U.S. national security,
worldwide energy security, the efficacy of multilateralism, and
the Nuclear Nonproliferation Treaty. Having defied the world
so brazenly, it might become overconfident enough to believe
that its conventional or proxy forces could operate without
fear of serious reprisals from the United States, Israel, or any
other power. It will be emboldened to use terrorism to threaten
or subvert others in the area—especially those who might be
inclined to pursue peace with Israel. Pro-Western Arab regimes such as Saudi Arabia, Egypt, and the gulf states sense
the Iranian threat, and if Iran succeeds in going nuclear, they
may decide to join Iran rather than fight it. And Iran, through
its support for Hezbollah and Hamas and the Baath Party in
Iraq, has the capacity to put direct pressure on Lebanon,
Syria, the Palestinians, and the Iraqis. Tens and perhaps hun-

dreds of thousands would join radical Islamist groups in the belief that Islamism is on the march.

Fundamentally, a nuclear Iran represents a unique threat. The fear of mutually assured destruction has long restrained other nuclear powers. There is a real risk that the Iranian leadership is not rational, that driven by its mad hatreds, it will act in ways that are unreasonable, even self-destructive. Anti-Americanism is a cornerstone of the ideology of this Islamic state. The virulence of Iran's hostility is impervious to reason. "Death to America!" has provoked the Iranian street for over a quarter of a century and is the venom upon which an entire generation of Iranians has been raised. The dominant Ayatollah Ali Khamenei reiterates that Iran's differences with America are more fundamental than political differences.

Whatever may happen to the leadership over time, the inescapable fact is that the United States just cannot take the risk of nuclear missiles in the hands of a clerical regime that preaches genocide. It is pathetic that appeasement continues to beguile.

Every U.S. administration since 1979—yes, including the past one—has reached out to the Iranians. To adopt President Obama's inaugural metaphor, every open hand has met a clenched fist. Jimmy Carter could not obtain the release of American hostages illegally seized in Tehran. Ronald Reagan's national security adviser, Robert McFarlane, failed in a secret mission to release the American hostages held by Iran's Hezbollah agents in Beirut. Brent Scowcroft, George H. W. Bush's national security adviser, made no progress. The Clinton administration's dozen gestures in 1999 were spurned. Clinton even lifted some sanctions in the interest of a "grand bargain," to be made public through an "accidental" meeting between Clinton and the Iranian president in the corridors of the United Nations, only to have it canceled at the last minute.

It is the same dismal story with five years of efforts to curb Iran's nuclear ambitions. "We haven't really moved one inch toward addressing the issues," said Mohamed ElBaradei, director general of the International Atomic Energy Agency. The lie to the Iranian pretense that this oil-rich country needs nuclear power is manifest in every action: It has refused every compromise, including Russia's offer to provide enriched nuclear material for use in civilian nuclear plants.

It is not that the Iranians don't want to talk—they do. That's how they play for time. Quite simply, they seek the technical know-how that will enable them to produce nuclear weapons in a short period. They are in the midst of building stockpiles of low-enriched uranium from which they can produce enough highly enriched uranium for a nuclear device in a matter of months—a breakout capability. They are adding centrifuges faster than the U.N. Security Council can step up the pressure and are learning about the intricate art of connecting a large number of centrifuges to a vast amount of pipe work, while maintaining everything in a vacuum. Getting centrifuges to run is not the challenge; getting them to run as a single entity is, and they are mastering it. Simultaneously, they are enhancing their ability to launch long-range ballistic missiles, a potential delivery system of nuclear weapons. Alas, this is also a living testimony to the failure of the world community to curb the trade of missile technology that Iran lacks on its own. What madness it is to empower Iran to do what it most likes to do—hold hostages, in this case, the entire region. The clock is ticking inexorably, a race against time that Iran is winning, getting nearer every day to presenting the world with an Iranian bomb as a *fait accompli*.

What can be done? Alas, the U.N. has failed to persuade countries like Russia and China to cooperate in a rigorous sanctions effort. Far from it, they are actually profiting from the sanctions' policy by doing deals in the energy field and selling Iran weapons. Russia and, to a lesser extent, China have made it clear they will block meaningful sanctions by the U.N.—even though effective economic sanctions and mea-

Iran's History of Non-Compliance with the Non-Proliferation Treaty

The Treaty on the Non-Proliferation of Nuclear Weapons, signed on 1 July 1968, calls for the safeguarding of peaceful nuclear activities. It obliges Iran to accept the Safeguard Agreement, which entered into force on 15 May 1974. The IAEA [International Atomic Energy Agency] prescribed it in order to ensure that Iran's nuclear program would be for peaceful energy, not for developing nuclear weapons. The international community must not impede Iran's right to research, develop and use nuclear energy for peaceful purposes.

The issue of Iranian non-compliance with the NPT [Non-Proliferation Treaty] arose when the deputy head of the Atomic Energy Organization of Iran, Said Esmail Khalilipour, sent a letter to the IAEA on October 9, 2003, stating that Iran had not been in compliance with its Safeguards Agreement since the early 1980s. Subsequent correspondence between Iran and the IAEA, as well as an IAEA visit to Iran, revealed the extent of the non-compliance.

This history of admitted non-compliance generated the current skepticism surrounding Iran's present compliance with the NPT.

Mark S. Williams,
"Iranian Non-Compliance with the IAEA,"
Peace Magazine, April–June 2009.

sures to isolate the regime may make the difference between a diplomatic deal and a nuclear standoff. But, to date, neither economic distress nor additional sanctions have changed the Iranian calculation.

Fortunately, Iran has an economic Achilles' heel: It is dependent on imported gasoline for 40 percent of its refined fuel. Furthermore, the country requires new investments in its energy industry to maintain current production. Reduced oil prices have put a great strain on its economy. Discontent is growing among a citizenry that is suffering from high inflation, unemployment, and poverty. Clearly, it makes sense to play on this fundamental weakness. We must press harder to coordinate four measures:

1. An arms embargo.

2. A ban on exports to Iran of gas and other refined products to cripple transport.

3. A global boycott of the entire banking system of Iran, instead of helping it as European banks are.

4. A prohibition on Western countries supplying spare parts to the oil industry.

The object, clearly, is not to punish the Iranian people but to force their leaders to act in the best interests of their people and of regional peace. It is the Iranian people who stand to gain the most from the cultural and economic liberations that would follow a sound agreement. And by that I mean a package deal that includes maximum safeguards and control of the nuclear program and the complete cessation of enrichment activities inside Iran: There is no combination of international inspections or co-ownership of enrichment facilities that would provide sufficient assurances that Iran is not producing weapons-grade missile material.

Before President Obama engages in "aggressive personal diplomacy," as he put it, he would be well advised to allow Iran's economic crisis to take its toll, in the hopes that an economic tailspin will leave the leadership more vulnerable to economic sanctions than it has been in the past 30 years and therefore more ready to come to terms. But there is no certainty that economic sanctions will work in time, leaving us with two unacceptable options: living with a nuclear Iran or acting militarily to prevent it.

The Iranian leaders' judgment is that the current administration is ready to let diplomacy run on and on and on ... and will anyway be incapable of making a military move while wrestling with the fallout from our domestic financial collapse. For this reason, many in Iran believe that the United States may be reconciling itself to the idea of living with an Iranian nuclear missile—even though it would be in the hands of an expressly genocidal regime.

Who would have imagined that President Obama may well determine his historical legacy and reputation on the basis of the way he deals with Iran?

> *"There are compelling theoretical and historical reasons to think that, far from being a crisis, Iranian membership in the nuclear club might be beneficial to everyone."*

A Nuclear Iran Is Not a Threat to the United States and Its Allies

Michael C. Desch

Many analysts and politicians have stated that Iran's possession of a nuclear weapon would be a catastrophic threat to the security of the United States, its allies, and the Middle East. In the viewpoint that follows, however, Michael C. Desch refutes this view and argues that a nuclear Iran could actually benefit the world by increasing security and limiting military aggression. Desch uses the Cold War theory of deterrence, which holds that countries possessing nuclear weapons will not engage other countries with nuclear weapons for fear of a nuclear retaliation, to support his view. He maintains that Iran is like the Soviet Union and China of that era, and that neither of these countries ever seriously considered using their nuclear weapons in an offensive attack against the United States or its allies due to fear of re-

Michael C. Desch, "Apocalypse Not," *The American Conservative*, vol. 8, May 18, 2009, pp. 6–8. Copyright © 2009 The American Conservative. Reproduced by permission.

prisal. Should Iran obtain nuclear weapons capabilities, Desch states that Iran's government would refrain from using a nuclear weapon in a first strike attack for the same reason. Desch is a political science professor and fellow of the Joan B. Kroc Institute for International Peace Studies at the University of Notre Dame. He is the author of Power and Military Effectiveness: The Fallacy of Democratic Triumphalism.

As you read, consider the following questions:

1. What historical evidence does Desch use to show that nuclear weapons make the countries that possess them "more careful" in their foreign relations with other nuclear powers?

2. How is the behavior of Cold War China and the Soviet Union similar to that of present day Iran, as stated by the author?

3. According to the author, does Iran behave as a rational actor, and what evidence does he use to support this claim?

The American Intelligence community has not yet concluded that Iran has even decided to develop a nuclear weapon, but the public debate has moved on to another question: what happens if it does?

Agreement About the Dangers of a Nuclear Iran

There is an overwhelming consensus that it would be an unmitigated disaster for the Islamic Republic of Iran to develop its nuclear program to the point that it could produce a weapon. As Israel's new prime minister, Benyamin Netanyahu, warned *The Atlantic*'s Jeffrey Goldberg, "You don't want a messianic apocalyptic cult controlling atomic bombs. When the wide-eyed believer gets hold of the reins of power and the weapons of mass death, then the entire world should start worrying, and that is what is happening in Iran."

Despite many disagreements with Netanyahu and his xenophobic foreign minister, Avigdor Lieberman, President [Barack] Obama shares the view that "there is no greater threat to Israel—or to the peace and stability of the region—than Iran." As he told the American Israel Public Affairs Committee while campaigning last May [2008],

> The Iranian regime supports violent extremists and challenges us across the region. It pursues a nuclear capability that could spark a dangerous arms race and raise the prospect of a transfer of nuclear know-how to terrorists. Its president denies the Holocaust and threatens to wipe Israel off the map. The danger from Iran is grave, it is real, and my goal will be to eliminate this threat.

To be sure, America's new Democratic president and Israel's new right-wing government have very different strategies for preventing Iran from going ballistic. Obama and much of the international community think that engagement with the Iranians is the best way to prevent the Persian Gulf doomsday clock from ticking down to zero. In contrast, many in Israel, and a significant number of the Jewish state's American supporters, believe that only the Gideon's sword of a preemptive military strike will end the mad mullahs' race to Armageddon.

Iran's Inferior Missiles Still Raise Fears

Of course, not everyone shares the apocalyptic rhetoric of the "strike-before-it's-too-late" crowd. Indeed, less fevered minds understand that even if Iran developed a rudimentary nuclear capability, the United States and Israel would have a huge missile advantage. According to the Federation of American Scientists, the U.S. has over 5,000 warheads deployed and a large number in reserve, while estimates of the Israeli stockpile range from 80 to 200 nuclear devices. At present, Iran has none and, even under worst-case scenarios, is unlikely to have more than a handful in the years to come.

Warheads without a way to deliver them aren't much use. In this respect, Iran is a nuclear pygmy: it has no long-range missiles that can reach the United States. Its medium-range missile capability, which can theoretically reach Israel, is unreliable. In contrast, the Center for Defense Information estimates that Israel has between 100 and 150 Jericho missiles, plus more than 200 F-4E Phantom and F-16 Falcon aircraft capable of delivering nuclear weapons. The United States has almost 1,500 nuclear delivery platforms, including Minuteman III and MX intercontinental ballistic missiles (ICBM's), Trident I and II submarine launched ballistic missiles (SLBM's), B-52H Stratofortress and B-2 Spirit long-range bombers, and a variety of tactical nuclear bombs and cruise missiles.

Still, even sophisticated analysts think that, on balance, an Iranian nuclear weapon would have deleterious, if not catastrophic, consequences. The concern is that once Iran develops a nuclear capability, it would become even more aggressive in supporting terrorist groups like Hezbollah in Lebanon or Hamas in Gaza. Another worry is that an Iranian bomb will set off a regional nuclear arms race. Finally, many Americans fear that once Iran fields a nuclear weapon, it will become even more meddlesome in Iraq. In other words, you don't have to think that an Iranian nuclear weapon is the end of the world to believe that it would be better for all concerned if [Iran's capital] Tehran never got one.

A Nuclear Iran Could Be Beneficial

Any time the conventional wisdom is so one-sided, it makes sense to ask whether it is truly wise or simply an unreasoning article of faith. What has been missing from the debate is a consideration of the possible benefits of Iran crossing the nuclear threshold. No doubt even this suggestion will strike many as the height of academic muddle-headedness. But there are compelling theoretical and historical reasons to think that, far from being a crisis, Iranian membership in the nuclear club might be beneficial to everyone—even Israel.

The theoretical basis for this admittedly counterintuitive claim is political scientist Kenneth Waltz's famous Adelphi Paper, "The Spread of Nuclear Weapons: More May Be Better." Waltz is not a marginal figure on the lunatic fringe, but rather ranks among the most influential international-relations theorists of the past 30 years. First published in 1981 by the prestigious International Institute for Strategic Studies in London—hardly a crackpot outfit—the paper argues that because nuclear weapons are only useful for deterrence of attacks upon their possessor's homeland, their proliferation, unlike that of other weapons that can be used for offensive operations, should reduce the frequency and intensity of wars. His central assumption is that rational states quickly realize this is the consequence of the nuclear revolution.

The Power of Deterrence

History has provided strong evidence that the development of nuclear weapons makes nuclear powers more careful, particularly in their relationships with each other. While there were many Cold War crises between the United States and the Soviet Union (and China), none escalated into major combat, much less all-out nuclear war. The same logic has apparently operated in the Indo-Pakistani relationship, the Kargil conflict of 1999 notwithstanding.

There is good evidence to suggest that the containment of these crises was the result of both sides stepping back from the brink of conflict for fear of unleashing a nuclear nightmare. Reflecting back on the Cuban Missile Crisis almost 30 years earlier, former secretary of defense Robert McNamara noted, "the lessons of the missile crisis are simple: Nuclear weapons are useful only for deterrence." Former [Soviet Union

Premier Nikita] Khrushchev aide Fyodor Burlatsky echoed this point, concluding, "it is impossible to win a nuclear war, and both sides realized that, maybe for the first time."

But for many participants in today's debate about the Iranian nuclear program, history is irrelevant because they think that the mullocracy in Iran is fundamentally different from the Cold War nuclear powers. They make two related arguments. First, Iran is an autocratic regime with little concern for the lives of its citizens, so it would not be deterred from nuclear war simply by the risk of suffering millions of casualties. Second, because Iran is a theocracy, it does not make rational strategic calculations, which are central to Waltz's theory.

Similarities Between Iran and Cold War Powers

Proponents of the first proposition suffer from historical amnesia. The first two nuclear adversaries the United States faced—[Josef] Stalin's Soviet Union and Mao [Zedong's] China—were hardly democratic regimes. Indeed, they rank among history's most totalitarian political systems. Yet neither of these totalitarian regimes risked nuclear war.

Both regimes engaged in mass murder of their own citizens. Conservative estimates of the human cost of Stalin's rule begin at 20 million deaths. Mao killed approximately the same number of his countrymen. Despite these sanguinary tendencies, neither regime was willing to risk nuclear war with the United States.

Both also indulged in irresponsible nuclear rhetoric. Stalin publicly pooh-poohed the American atomic bomb when told about it by President [Harry] Truman at Potsdam in July 1945. Behind the scenes, however, he understood that atomic weapons represented a dramatic change in the nature of warfare and secretly began a crash program. The rhetoric of cava-

Understanding Iran's Nuclear Program

Iran now has a stockpile of low-enriched uranium. To enrich this to weapons-grade capability it has to run it through its existing centrifuges until the appropriate levels (about 93 per cent) are reached, though this is not easy. In 1989, [then president, Ali Akbar Hashemi] Rafsanjani might have wished for a nuclear deterrent, but it was impossible. Iran does not yet have the bomb. The country does not want the international isolation that would follow its attainment, but it could be pushed: military attack would accelerate a weapons drive from Tehran [Iran's capital].

The [George W.] Bush administration believed Tehran's nuclear ambitions were a barrier to dialogue. They shouldn't have been. The nuclear stand-off is not the cause, but the effect of a wider problem, and it is a political one. Barack Obama has made détente [the opening of dialogue through diplomacy] with the Islamic Republic his most audacious hope yet. However, to deal with Iran, we must first understand it. The nuclear programme offers us this chance.

The nuclear programme is many things to Iran but most of all it is the expression of a nation seeking a place in the modern world. It is an irony, and a peculiarly Iranian one, that it pursues the one thing that may bring its total isolation from what it wants above all else: acceptance—but on its own terms.

David Patri Karakos,
"How Iran Went Nuclear,"
New Statesman, *June 22, 2009, p. 33.*

lier dismissal concealed a deep concern about nuclear weapons that, in turn, induced caution.

During his 1957 speech at the Moscow Meeting of Communist and Workers' Parties, Mao also dismissed the nuclear-armed United States as "a paper tiger" and remarked elsewhere that a nuclear war with the U.S. would not be such a catastrophe because "if worse came to worst and half of mankind died, the other half would remain while imperialism would be razed to the ground and the whole world would become socialist." But in private conversations with Field Marshal Sir Bernard Law Montgomery in September 1961, he argued that nuclear weapons "are not something to use. The more there are, the harder it will be for nuclear wars to break out." This latter view apparently governed Chinese behavior.

Iran's Consistency and Rationality

The second objection to Waltz's nuclear optimism is that Iran will not behave as a rational actor because it is an Islamic theocracy that values the afterlife more than the here and now. True, revolutionary Iran fought an eight-year war with Iraq and suffered almost a million casualties. But this is hardly evidence that its leadership and population have a martyrdom complex. It was, after all, secular Iraq, rather than Iran, that started the war, and the Islamic Republic was the first to accept the United Nations' ceasefire in 1988 once it became clear that the conflict had reached a stalemate. This behavior hardly indicates an irrational commitment to fight to the last Iranian.

There is no doubt that the rhetoric of some Iranian leaders, particularly President Mahmoud Ahmadinejad's florid threats that Israel will be "wiped off the map" and his ludicrous denials of the Holocaust, has been inflammatory and irresponsible. Yet we need to keep in mind that Iran is a much more complex political system than most Western media accounts suggest, and its president is not the most significant political actor in that country.

More importantly, when one looks systematically at recent Iranian history, as Trita Parsi [president of the National Iranian American Council] has done in his essential *Treacherous Alliance: The Secret Dealings of Israel, Iran, and the U.S.*, two things become clear. Iranian behavior toward the United States and Israel has been remarkably consistent, both before and after the Islamic Revolution. That continuity is largely explained by a realpolitik not so different from the logic that informed the policies of the Cold War superpowers.

At various times under both the Shah and the mullahs [religious leaders], Iran sought regional hegemony; at other times, under both regimes, it made overtures to the United States and even to Israel. Thus there is little reason to think that Iran would behave any differently than the Soviet Union or Communist China with nuclear weapons. If we could live with those rogue nuclear states, which were willing to sacrifice millions of their own people to advance an eschatological ideology, there is scant reason to think Iran poses a more serious threat.

The Stabilizing Effect of a Nuclear Iran

One could go further and suggest that a nuclear Iran might even be beneficial to the United States. The nuclear stalemate played an important role in American efforts to contain the Soviet Union, and containment, in turn, had the effect of "mellowing" the regime, as [American diplomat and political scientist] George Kennan predicted in his famous *Foreign Affairs* article ["The Sources of Soviet Conduct"]. Why should we not expect a regional stalemate involving the United States, Israel, and Iran to have a similar effect by simultaneously bolstering each nation's territorial security without providing any of them with the means of conquest against other states?

Arguing that an Iranian nuclear capability could benefit Israel is admittedly a more controversial claim. But in addition to the possible mellowing of the Iranian political system, which would be a long-term benefit for Israeli security, there could be some immediate payoffs, too. A nuclear Iran would certainly change the dynamics of the Persian Gulf, with many Arab states desperately searching for a nuclear ally to balance against Iran. Aside from the United States, Israel is the only counterweight in the region. A nuclear Iran could warm relations between Israel and moderate Arab states throughout the region who regard a powerful Iran—Islamic or not—as a threat.

I'm not arguing that an Iranian nuclear deterrent would have immediate transformative effects. It certainly would not, as more than 40 years of Cold War crises demonstrate. I also concede that the ideal situation would be a world without conflict in which nuclear weapons would be unnecessary. But we don't live in that world. And so I am led to conclude, based upon our best theory of international relations and the perspective of Cold War history, that an Iranian nuclear deterrent would solve more problems than it creates. To paraphrase the subtitle of [director] Stanley Kubrick's great nuclear satire [film] *Dr. Strangelove*, it might just be time to stop worrying and learn, if not to love, at least to tolerate the Iranian bomb.

> "The Iranian terrorist threat is especially dangerous since it threatens key United States security interests and American citizens alike."

Iran Is a State Sponsor of Terrorism

Matthew A. Levitt

In the following viewpoint, Matthew A. Levitt expounds on the numerous examples of Iranian state sponsored terrorism. Levitt argues that due to its sheer scope, the Iranian funding, training, and general aiding of terrorism worldwide presents a unique threat to the United States and its allies. By tracing a multitude of examples, the author makes the case that the state sponsorship of terror by Iran has provided global terrorist cells, including Hezbollah in Lebanon and Hamas in Palestine, with the means necessary to harm American citizens both at home and abroad. Levitt is director of the Stein Program on Counterterrorism and Intelligence at the Washington Institute for Near East Policy.

Matthew A. Levitt, "Iranian State Sponsorship of Terror: Threatening U.S. Security, Global Stability, and Regional Peace," Joint Hearing of the Committee on International Relations Subcommittee on Middle East and Central Asia, and the Subcommittee on International Terrorism and Nonproliferation, United States House of Representatives, February 16, 2005. Reproduced by permission of the author.

As you read, consider the following questions:

1. As reported in the viewpoint, how much money did Western diplomats and analysts in Lebanon estimate that Hezbollah receives from Iran annually?

2. As stated by Levitt, what is the "best documented example of the operational relationship" between Iran and Hezbollah?

3. What is Al-Manar, and how does Iran aid this entity, according to the author?

CIA [Central Intelligence Agency] officials regularly describe Iran as "the foremost state sponsor of terror." President [George W.] Bush reaffirmed this assessment in his recent [2005] State of the Union address, saying, "Today, Iran remains the world's primary state sponsor of terror." And earlier this month [February 2005], British Prime Minister Tony Blair echoed the U.S. government's perception of Iran, saying Iran "certainly does sponsor terrorism. There is no doubt about that at all."

The Scope of Iran's Terrorist Involvement

To be sure, Iran's support for Lebanese Hezbollah [an Islamist political and paramilitary organization] alone justifies these conclusions. Hezbollah, a U.S.-designated terrorist organization, was responsible for more American deaths than any other terrorist organization until September 11 [2001, when thousands died in terrorist attacks in the United States perpetrated by al-Qaeda]. Highlights of Hezbollah's record of terror attacks include suicide truck bombings targeting U.S. and French forces in Beirut (in 1983 and 1984) and U.S. forces again in Saudi Arabia (in 1996), its record of suicide bombing attacks targeting Jewish and Israeli interests such as those in Argentina (1992 and 1994) and in Thailand (attempted in 1994), and a host of other plots targeting American, French,

German, British, Kuwaiti, Bahraini and other interests in plots from Europe to Southeast Asia to the Middle East.

According to U.S. authorities, concern over the threat posed by Hezbollah is well placed. FBI [Federal Bureau of Investigation] officials testified before the Senate Select Committee on Intelligence in February 2002 that "FBI investigations to date continue to indicate that many Hezbollah subjects based in the United States have the capability to attempt terrorist attacks here should this be a desired objective of the group." Similarly, CIA Director George Tenet testified before the Senate Armed Services Committee in February 2003 that "Hezbollah, as an organization with capability and worldwide presence, is [al-Qaeda's] equal, if not a far more capable organization." That capability is a direct result of Hezbollah's intimate ties to—and training at the hands of—Iranian security and intelligence services.

Iran's terrorist activities can be split into several primary categories. First, Iran actively seeks to undermine prospects for Israeli-Arab peace. Second, Iran sponsors terrorist groups of global reach, including funding, training, arming and providing safe haven to their members. Third, Iranian intelligence operatives are themselves engaged in terrorist activity on their own and in cooperation with terrorist groups, including surveillance of U.S. interests at home and abroad. This includes efforts to destabilize regimes not to [Iran's capital] Tehran's liking, particularly in the Middle East, as evidenced most recently by Iranian activity in Iraq. . . .

Funding Terrorism Against Israel

Iran has long been believed to fund Hezbollah to the tune of at least $100 million per year. Recently, Western diplomats and analysts in Lebanon estimated Hezbollah receives closer to $200 million a year from Iran. The increase is likely due to Iran's keen interest in undermining prospects for Israeli-Palestinian peace (and, in general, further destabilizing the

Israeli-Palestinian conflict), and Hezbollah's growing role as Iran's proxy to achieve this goal. Hezbollah's success in funding and training Palestinian groups may well explain the increase in funding since Iran is known to employ a results-oriented approach to determining the level of funding it is willing to provide terrorist groups. As a U.S. court noted in *Weinstein v. Iran*, the period of 1995–1996 "was a peak period for Iranian economic support of Hamas [another Islamist organization] because Iran typically paid for results, and Hamas was providing results by committing numerous bus bombings." Iranian funding to terrorist groups like Hamas and Islamic Jihad (most often funneled via Hezbollah) increases when they carry out successful attacks and decreases when they fail, are thwarted or are postponed due to ceasefires or other political considerations. Unlike most terrorist groups, which need to focus much time and attention on raising, laundering and transferring funds, Iran's largesse provides Hezbollah with a sizable and constant flow of reliable funding. By all accounts, Hezbollah operates under no revenue constraints; indeed, it often serves as a middleman funneling funds from Iran to other terrorist groups such as the Palestinian Islamic Jihad (PIJ), Fatah Tanzim, and others.

Iran actively supports Hezbollah's involvement in the Palestinian-Israeli conflict and its support of Palestinian militants. U.S. officials contend that, shortly after Palestinian violence erupted in September 2000, Iran assigned Imad Mughniyeh, Hezbollah's international operations commander, to help Palestinian militant groups, specifically Hamas and PIJ. Mughniyeh features prominently on the FBI list of most wanted terrorists, and is the subject of a sealed U.S. indictment for his role in the 1985 TWA hijacking [a Trans World Airlines hijacking carried out by Lebanese Shia Islamists where passengers were held hostage for two weeks, and one was killed]. According to a former [President Bill] Clinton administration official, "Mughniyeh got orders from Tehran to work with Hamas." In fact, in the March 27, 2002, "Passover massacre" suicide bombing, Hamas relied on the guidance of a Hezbollah expert to build an extra-potent bomb. . . .

Iran Trains Terrorists

On top of funding terrorist groups targeting Israel and the peace process, Iranian training camps run by Hezbollah and the Popular Front for the Liberation of Palestine-General Command (PFLP-GC) dot the Syrian and Lebanese landscapes, where Hezbollah and Iranian trainers have schooled a motley crew of Palestinian, Kurdish, Armenian, and other recruits in a variety of terrorist and intelligence tactics. For example, several of the terrorists who carried out the 1996 Khobar Towers bombing [in Saudi Arabia in which 20 people were killed and another 372 were wounded] were recruited in Syria and trained in Hezbollah camps in Lebanon and Iran.

Palestinian legislator and scholar Ziad Abu-Amr notes that Iran provides "logistical support to Hamas and military training to its members." According to a Canadian intelligence report, "Hamas has training camps in Iran, Lebanon, and Sudan. Hamas camps in Lebanon are said to be under Iranian supervision."

Perhaps the best known case of Iranian agents training Palestinian terrorists is the case of Hassan Salamah, the Hamas commander who was the mastermind behind the string of suicide bus bombings carried out by Hamas in February and March 1996. Both in his statements to Israeli police and an interview on CBS's *60 Minutes*, Salamah noted that after undergoing ideological indoctrination training in Sudan he was sent to Syria and from there transported to Iran on an Iranian aircraft to a base near Tehran. Osama Hamdan, Hamas's representative to Iran at the time, met Salamah in Tehran, after which Salamah underwent three months of military training at the hands of Iranian trainers. With the help of a translator (Salamah did not speak Farsi and his trainers did not speak Arabic well), Salamah trained to use explosives, automatic weapons, hand grenades, shoulder-fired missiles, ambush techniques, how to deactivate land mines and extract their explosive material, and how to build trigger mechanisms for bombs. By his own statement, Salamah received all his military training in Iran. . . .

The Iranian Supply of Weapons

Iran also ships and smuggles weapons to a variety of terrorist groups. Iranian cargo planes deliver sophisticated weaponry, from rockets to small arms, to Hezbollah in regular flights to Damascus [the capital of Syria] from Tehran. These weapons are offloaded in Syria and trucked to Hezbollah camps in Lebanon's Beka'a Valley. In January 2004, Iran reportedly took advantage of the international humanitarian aid effort to assist earthquake victims in Iran to supply weapons to Hezbollah. Cargo planes reportedly flew to Iran from Syria filled with aid supplies, and returned full of weapons for Hezbollah.

Iranian involvement in the *Karine-A* weapons smuggling ship—intercepted by the Isareli Navy in the Red Sea in January 2002—is well documented. The White House described evidence of Iran's role in the *Karine-A* incident as "compelling," a conclusion echoed in the statements of Director of Central Intelligence Tenet, senior State Department officials, and even European officials. Speaking before the European Parliament in Strasbourg in February 2002, European Union head of foreign affairs Javier Solana described the *Karine-A* as "the link between Iran and the PA [Palestinian National Authority]," adding that "such a connection had not existed for many years." Hezbollah's role in the affair is also well known. Not only did Iran arrange for Hezbollah external operations commander Imad Mughniyeh to purchase the *Karine-A*, but Mughniyeh's deputy, Haj Bassem, personally commanded the ship that met the *Karine-A* at the island of Kish (south of Iran) and oversaw the ship-to-ship transfer of the Iranian weapons. . . .

Iran's Direct Involvement in Terrorism

Iranian agents have long been directly involved in acts of terrorism themselves and in concert with Hezbollah networks, beyond the terrorist activities carried out independently by the proxy groups sponsored by Tehran. One of the earliest cases on which information is publicly available is the German indictment of Iran's then-intelligence minister in 1997 in the infamous "Mykonos case." Two Iranian intelligence officers and two Hezbollah operatives carried out the assassination of four leaders of the Democratic Party of Iranian Kurdistan (DPIK), an Iranian dissident group. To be sure, one of the most significant *modus operandi* [Latin phrase meaning methods of operating] that runs through all of Hezbollah's global activities—financial, logistical and operational—is that at some level all Hezbollah networks are overseen by, and are in contact with, senior Hezbollah leaders in Lebanon and/or Iranian officials. . . .

Perhaps the best documented example of the operational relationship Iran maintains with Hezbollah is Tehran's role in the bombing of the Buenos Aires Jewish community center (Asociacion Mutual Israelita Argentina, or AMIA). According to Abdolghassem Mesbahi, a high-level Iranian defector, the decision to bomb the AMIA building was made at a meeting of senior Iranian decision makers on August 14, 1993. The meeting reportedly included the Supreme Leader Ali Hoseini Khamenei, former President Ali Akbar Hashemi, Rafsanjani, former Foreign Minister Ali Akbar Vlayati, the Head of Intelligence and Security in Khamenei's Bureau, Mohammed Hjazi, former Intelligence Minister Ali Fallahian, and Iranian secret service agent Mohsen Rabbani. According to Argentinean court documents, the Argentinean intelligence service (SIDE) believes that Khameini issued a *fatwa* [religious opinion] concerning AMIA. This *fatwa* was then handed down from Fallahian to Imad Mughniyeh, the "special operations" chief of Hezbollah. Mughniyeh worked in conjunction with Rabbani, who was able to help orchestrate the plan for the bombing clandestinely under the guise of heading the Iranian Cultural Bureau at the Iranian Embassy in Buenos Aires. Rabbani attempted to buy a *Renault-Trafic* model van, the same model that was used in the bombing, and is suspected of being involved with several commercial activities through fictitious or undercover enterprises on behalf of Iranian intelligence. Investigators also uncovered records of phone calls between the Iranian embassy in Buenos Aires and suspected Hezbollah operatives in the triborder area who operated out of a mosque and a travel agency there.

According to expert opinions included in the Argentinean court document, it is well known that Hezbollah operatives often receive training in Iran. In addition, Hezbollah prefers outside operatives to local contacts when running its major operations in other countries. These operatives generally are more trustworthy and better trained. The terrorists that conducted the AMIA bombing would have had greater difficulty operating without the operational support of Iran, which reportedly included the bribing of then Argentinean President Carlos Menem with a payment of $10 million dollars to keep Iran's involvement quiet. . . .

Iranian Ties to al-Qaeda

While the 9/11 Commission found no evidence that Iran or Hezbollah had advance knowledge of the September 11 [2001] plot [to hijack and crash airplanes into major U.S. sites], the commission's report does note that Iran and Hezbollah provided assistance to al-Qaeda on several occasions. For example, al-Qaeda operatives were allowed to travel through Iran with great ease. Entry stamps were not put in Saudi operatives' passports at the border, though at least eight of the September 11 hijackers transited the country between October 2000 and February 2001. The report also noted a "persistence of contacts between Iranian security officials and senior al-

The Iranian Effort to Destabilize Iraq

The Qods Force, an elite branch of the Islamic Revolutionary Guard Corps (IRGC), is the regime's primary mechanism for cultivating and supporting terrorists abroad. The Qods Force provided aid in the form of weapons, training, and funding to HAMAS and other Palestinian terrorist groups, Lebanese Hizballah, Iraq-based militants, and Taliban fighters in Afghanistan. . . .

Despite its pledge to support the stabilization of Iraq, Iranian authorities continued to provide lethal support, including weapons, training, funding, and guidance, to Iraqi militant groups that targeted Coalition and Iraqi forces and killed innocent Iraqi civilians. Iran's Qods Force continued to provide Iraqi militants with Iranian-produced advanced rockets, sniper rifles, automatic weapons, and mortars that have killed Iraqi and Coalition Forces as well as civilians. Tehran [Iran's capital] was responsible for some of the lethality of anti-Coalition attacks by providing militants with the capability to assemble improvised explosive devices (IEDs) with explosively formed projectiles (EFPs) that were specially designed to defeat armored vehicles. The Qods Force, in concert with Lebanese Hizballah, provided training both inside and outside of Iraq for Iraqi militants in the construction and use of sophisticated IED technology and other advanced weaponry.

Office of the Coordinator for Counterterrorism,
"State Sponsors of Terrorism,"
Country Reports on Terrorism 2008, *April 30, 2009.*

Qaeda figures" and drew attention to an informal agreement by which Iran would support al-Qaeda training with the understanding that such training would be used "for actions carried out primarily against Israel and the United States." Indeed, al-Qaeda operatives were trained in explosives, security, and intelligence on at least two occasions, with one group trained in Iran around 1992, and a second trained by Hezbollah in Lebanon's Beka'a Valley in the fall of 1993.

Hezbollah depends on a wide variety of criminal enterprises, ranging from smuggling to fraud to drug trade to diamond trade in regions across the world, including North America, South America, and the Middle East, to raise money to support Hezbollah activities. Published reports suggest that al-Qaeda and Hezbollah have formed tactical, ad-hoc alliances with a variety of terrorist organizations to cooperate on money laundering and other unlawful activities. . . .

Iran's Support for Fundamentalist Propaganda

Beyond training and arming Hezbollah, Iran bankrolls the group's well-oiled propaganda machine as well. Al-Manar is the official television mouthpiece of Hezbollah, and is used by Hezbollah and Iran to radicalize Muslim youth and glorify violence, especially in the contexts of Israel and Iraq. Called the "station of resistance"—it serves as Hezbollah's tool to reach the entire Arab Muslim world to disseminate propaganda and promote terrorist activity. Al-Manar glorifies suicide bombings, calls for attacks targeting Israel, coalition forces in Iraq, and the United States, and seeks to create a radicalized constituency that is as likely to seek out terrorist groups themselves to join their ranks as they are to be sought after and recruited by these groups.

At the time of al-Manar's founding in 1991, the station reportedly received seed money from Iran and had a running budget of $1 million. By 2002 its annual budget had grown to approximately $15 million. Middle East analysts and journalists maintain that most of this funding comes from Iran. Avi

Jorisch, author of *Beacon of Hatred: Inside Hezbollah's al-Manar Television*, writes that "Iran provides an estimated $100–200 million per year to Hezbollah, which in turn transfers money to al-Manar, making Iranian funding of the station indirect." This was confirmed by former al-Manar program director Sheikh Nasir al-Akhdar who asserted that al-Manar receives a large portion of its budget through subsidies offered by Hezbollah.

According to one official in al-Manar's Art Graphic Department, al-Manar's music videos are meant to "help people on the way to committing what you call in the West a suicide mission. [They are] meant to be the first step in the process of a freedom fighter operation."

The United States has been a primary target of al-Manar programming and is depicted as a global oppressor. In a speech broadcast on al-Manar, Hezbollah Secretary-general Hassan Nasrallah stated, "Our enmity to the Great Satan is complete and unlimited. . . . Our echoing slogan will remain: Death to America!" One video features an altered image of the Statue of Liberty. The statue's head has been transformed into a skull with hollow eyes, her gown dripping in blood. Instead of a torch, she holds a sharp knife. After asserting that the United States "has pried into the affairs of most countries in the world," the video ends with the slogan, "America owes blood to all of humanity." . . .

The Consequences of Allowing Iranian-Sponsored Terrorism to Continue

Iran is indeed the world's foremost state sponsor of terrorism. The sheer scope of Iranian terrorist activity is remarkable, including both the terrorism carried out by Iranian-supported terrorist groups and by Iranian agents themselves. But the Iranian terrorist threat is especially dangerous since it threatens key United States security interests and American citizens alike.

First, Iran and its proxies present a direct threat to the United States both at home and abroad, including U.S. and coalition forces overseas. Consider the Iranian security personnel caught surveilling targets in New York. Second, Iran, along with its primary proxy, Hezbollah, is the single most dangerous threat to the prospects of securing Arab-Israeli peace. Consider Palestinian fears that Iran and Hezbollah are actively trying to torpedo the nascent ceasefire and possibly assassinate Palestinian president Mahmoud Abbas. Third, Iran is fully engaged in undermining coalition efforts in Iraq. Note the infiltration of Iranian agents and the recent announcement that eighteen Hezbollah members have been arrested there.

It is critical that the international effort to rein in Iran's nuclear weapons program include an equally concerted effort to forestall its state sponsorship of terrorism. Failure to do so guarantees Iran and its proxies will continue to undermine Israeli-Arab peace negotiations, conduct surveillance of U.S., Israeli and other targets for possible terrorist attack, and destabilize Iraq.

> *"Iran's past behavior suggests it is not likely to provide chemical, biological, radiological, or nuclear weapons to a terrorist group."*

Iran Will Not Provide Terrorists with Weapons of Mass Destruction

Daniel Byman

Much of the fear surrounding Iran's attainment of nuclear weapons is based on the concern that Iran would pass these capabilities on to the terrorist groups it supports. Daniel Byman argues in the following viewpoint, however, that Iran's history of terrorist support actually shows that it would not provide terrorists with weapons of mass destruction (WMDs). Byman carefully examines the inception of Iran's state sponsorship of terrorism as well as the country's means of supporting terrorism throughout its history. In doing so, he comes to the conclusion that Iran would incur limited or no benefits by arming terrorists with WMDs, and therefore, would not do so. Byman is the director of the Center for Peace and Security Studies at Georgetown Univer-

Daniel Byman, "Iran, Terrorism, and Weapons of Mass Destruction," *Studies in Conflict & Terrorism*, vol. 31, March 2008, pp. 169–72, 175–76, 178–79. Copyright © 2008 Taylor & Francis Group, LLC. Reproduced by permission of Taylor & Francis, Ltd., http://www.tandf.co.uk/journals and the author.

sity and a senior fellow on foreign policy at the Saban Center for Middle East Policy at the Brookings Institution, a public policy think tank.

As you read, consider the following questions:

1. For what three reasons does Daniel Byman believe Iran will not transfer WMDs to terrorist groups?

2. How, according to the author, has Iran been a "source of restraint on its proxies"?

3. As stated by Byman, how have the terrorist attacks of September 11, 2001, had a limiting effect on Iran's support of terrorism?

Since the Islamic Revolution in 1979, Iran has been one of the world's most active sponsors of terrorism. Tehran [Iran's capital] has armed, trained, financed, inspired, organized, and otherwise supported dozens of violent groups over the years. Iran has backed not only groups in its Persian Gulf neighborhood, but also terrorists and radicals in Lebanon, the Palestinian territories, Bosnia, the Philippines, and elsewhere. This support remains strong even today: the U.S. government regularly contends that Iran is tied to an array of radical groups in Iraq.

Yet despite Iran's very real support for terrorism for more than the last 25 years and its possession of chemical weapons for over 15 years, Tehran has not transferred unconventional systems to terrorists. Iran is likely to continue this restraint and not transfer chemical, biological, or nuclear weapons for several reasons. First, providing terrorists with such unconventional weapons offers Iran few tactical advantages as these groups are able to operate effectively with existing methods and weapons. Second, Iran has become more cautious in its backing of terrorists in recent years. And third, it is highly aware that any major escalation in its support for terrorism would incur U.S. wrath and international condemnation....

Exporting Revolution with Terrorism

Iran initially began supporting radical groups, including many that embraced terrorism, after the 1979 Islamic revolution [in which Iran's then monarchial leader Shah Mohammad Reza Pahlavi was over-thrown and replaced by Ayatollah Ruhollah Khomeini and the Islamic Republic] and quickly became the world's leading state supporter of terrorism. Exporting the revolution was a leading foreign policy goal, an ambition that led Tehran to work with a range of radicals around the world. The clerical regime in Tehran viewed supporting revolutions overseas as part of its revolutionary duty. The theological justifications for the Iranian revolution espoused by the clerics emphasized the spread of Islam regardless of state boundaries. Iran's Supreme Leader Ayatollah Khomeini, shortly after taking power, declared, "We should try hard to export our revolution to the world . . . we [shall] confront the world with our ideology." Indeed, Iran's constitution calls on its military forces to "extend the sovereignty of God's law throughout the world."

For Iran's new leaders, supporting Islam meant supporting revolution. Typifying a view common to revolutionary regimes, Iran's leaders saw themselves on the defensive yet believed that aggressively promoting their revolution was the best means of ensuring its survival. Ayatollah Khomeini declared that "[A]ll the superpowers and the [great] powers have risen to destroy us. If we remain in an enclosed environment we shall definitely face defeat." Heady with their own success against the Shah at home, Iranian leaders made no secret of their belief that "corrupt" and "illegitimate" leaders abroad such as Iraq's Saddam Hussain, the Al Saud family in Saudi Arabia, and others, would soon fall as well.

Immediately following the revolution, Tehran was particularly active in working with Shi'a Muslim movements around the world. As representatives of the world's largest Shi'a nation, Iranian leaders feel a special affinity for the world's Shi'a. In most countries in the Muslim world the Shi'a faced oppression and discrimination, and the revolution both inspired them to take action and to look to Tehran for support. Iran thus backed Shi'a groups in Iraq, Bahrain, Saudi Arabia, Pakistan, Kuwait, and elsewhere.

In the eyes of its founders, however, the Iranian revolution was more than simply a Shi'a movement. Tehran saw itself as the champion of the "dispossessed" around the world. Thus it embraced an array of left-wing revolutionary movements, many of which had secular ideologies.

Iran's Actions Spark Regional Hostility

Not surprisingly, this ideological support engendered considerable hostility among Iran's neighbors. They regularly condemned Iran, froze or cut trade, formed anti-Iran alliances, welcomed Iranian dissidents (including several groups that supported terrorism against Iran) and took other steps designed to weaken and isolate the new regime. Thus emerged a strategic rivalry between Iran and many of its neighbors in which terrorism and support for subversion were the major Iranian weapons in its toolbox.

For Iran, supporting subversive movements became a way of weakening and destabilizing its neighbors as well as spreading its revolution and toppling what in the eyes of Tehran were illegitimate regimes. In 1981, shortly after the outbreak of the Iranian revolution, Tehran aided Shi'a radicals of the Islamic Front for the Liberation of Bahrain in an attempted coup against Bahrain's ruling Al Khalifa family.

Iran took a similar approach in its support for the Supreme Council of the Islamic Revolution in Iraq. On taking power, Iranian leaders held a visceral loathing of Saddam Hussein's regime in Iraq—a hatred reinforced by [Iraq's capital] Baghdad's immediate execution of several prominent Shi'a religious leaders out of fear that they might support an Iranian-style movement in Iraq itself. Almost immediately after the revolution, Iran began supporting radicalism in Iraq, a decision that contributed to Baghdad's decision to invade Iran in 1980. As the war heated up, Khomeini declared that the path to Jerusalem's liberation went through Baghdad. In November 1982 Tehran organized various Iraqi Shi'ite groups under the umbrella of the Supreme Assembly for the Islamic Revolution in Iraq (SCIRI). SCIRI was more than just a guerrilla front to weaken Saddam's Iraq or an organization trying to kill Iraqi leaders: it was also a government-in-waiting. As Iran expert R.K. Ramazani contends, Iran's goal was to "undermine the Hussein regime and pave the way for the establishment of an Iranian-type Islamic government in Iraq."

Terrorism Gives Iran a Voice

In addition to giving Iran a way to weaken its neighbors, terrorism allowed Iran to influence events well beyond its borders. Lacking aircraft carriers or other military forces that can deploy thousands of miles away, and with its economy too weak to force far-away countries to heed their demands, Iranian political protests have often gone unheeded. Iran has used support for terrorists to project power, particularly in the Arab-Israeli arena but also against Iraqi targets and in Europe. Up until the early 1990s, Iranian intelligence services also assassinated Iranian dissidents in Europe.

Iran supported terrorist groups not only to weaken adversaries, but also to have a voice in the opposition to a particular regime. For example, after the Israeli invasion of Lebanon and the subsequent U.S. and European troop deployments there, Iran chose to undermine the existing Shi'a group, Amal, because it had cooperated with Israel. It is interesting to note that Iran chose to do so even though the organization was well-established and popular. To undermine Amal, Iranian intelligence agents, diplomats, and members of the Islamic Revolutionary Guard Corps (as well as Syrian officials) created the Lebanese Hizballah from a motley assortment of small Shi'ite organizations. Iran helped the fledgling movement train and indoctrinate new members in the Bekaa Valley and developed an entire infrastructure there to support it, including social services and a fundraising network. This effort paid off with the creation of a loyal and effective proxy. As one senior Hizballah official noted in the early 1980s, "Our relation with the Islamic revolution [in Iran] is one of a junior to a senior . . . of a soldier to his commander."

Domestic politics also motivate Iran to support radical groups. During the 1980s, Iran provided support to a range of Shi'a Muslim groups such as the Iraqi Dawa party, the Islamic Front for the Liberation of Bahrain, and the Tehrik-e Jafariya-e Pakistan in part because the regime's legitimacy also depended on its self-proclaimed status as the protector of Muslims, particularly Shi'as, worldwide. Bolstering this position required clear gestures of support.

The prestige garnered from support to radicals mattered abroad as well. After the 1979 Islamic revolution, both Saudi Arabia and Iran competed to champion Muslim causes as a form of influence. Iran saw its support for radical groups as a way of demonstrating its *bona fides* [Latin term meaning "in good faith" or good intentions] to other Islamist revolutionaries. . . .

Terrorism as Deterrence

Iran's use of terrorism has changed dramatically since the 1980s. Most importantly from a U.S. point of view, Iran appears not to target Americans directly, although it still retains the capability to do so and in Iraq some groups with links to Iran have fought with coalition forces. Iran instead uses terrorism as a form of deterrence, "casing" U.S. embassies and other facilities to give it a response should the United States step up pressure. Tehran also dramatically cut back on operations in Europe and the Gulf states since the early 1990s. Iranian officials feared that attacks on Iranian dissidents there would lead to European support for sanctions and reduce in-

Iran's Ascendance in the Middle East

Holding sway over a third of the Middle East and black-mailing 55 percent of the world's oil reserves, Iran is looking more and more like a superpower. [Its capital] Tehran has not achieved this through classic imperialism—invasion and occupation—but rather through a three-pronged strategy of proxy warfare, asymmetrical weapons and an appeal to the Middle East's downtrodden. If Tehran's ascendance continues, it will not be a rising China or Russia that challenges the United States for global supremacy—it will be Iran.

Right now, Tehran's proxy in Lebanon, Hezbollah, is the de facto state. With friendly governments in Damascus and Baghdad, Iran intends to put the rest of the Levant under its thumb. The power of America's traditional allies, Saudi Arabia, Jordan and Egypt, is diminishing at a time when Iranian influence is spreading across the Palestinian territories and the Gulf sheikhdoms. Iran is quietly but inexorably building an empire, securing territory, resources, raw economic power, military strength and the allegiance of the "oppressed." If Iran's rise continues, it will find itself at the heart of Middle East oil and at the apex of power.

Robert Baer, "Iranian Resurrection,"
National Interest, *November–December 2008.*

vestment in Iran's economy. In the mid-1990s, Iran's then President Ali Akbar Hashemi Rafsanjani engineered a rapprochement with the Arabian Gulf states, which led Iran to stop actively trying to overthrow those regimes, though it retains ties to a number of Shi'a groups there. Taken together, these three shifts represent a dramatic change in Iran's support for terrorism.

Today, Iran uses terrorism and support for radicals in several distinct ways. Particularly important for the United States are Tehran's close relationship with the Lebanese Hizballah; support for anti-Israel Palestinian groups; ties to various factions within Iraq; and loose contacts with Al Qaeda [terrorist organization responsible for the September 11, 2001, attacks]. . . .

Iran as a Source of Restraint

Although Iran has cut ties to terrorist groups in the Gulf and Europe, it retains a wide network and contacts with many radicals in these countries. Such contacts provide Iranian officials with options should they seek to use terrorism in these areas again. Moreover, these ties are a deterrent, allowing Tehran to tacitly threaten the United States or other countries that might seek to act against the clerical regime.

Although Iran's support for terrorists groups have made them more lethal (particularly with regard to Hizballah), Tehran is also a source of restraint on its proxies. Most importantly, Tehran takes seriously the threat of escalation from Israel, the United States, or other potential victims should its proxies wreak massive violence. Iran stopped supporting attacks by Gulf Shi'a on U.S. forces in the Persian Gulf after the 1996 Khobar Towers bombing [in Saudi Arabia that killed 17 American troops]—despite a continued desire to expel Americans from the region—in part because it feared an increase in political, economic, and perhaps even military pressure. After the bombing, Iranian leaders worried they might have crossed the line they had long walked between confrontation and provocation. Similarly, Iran did not let the SCIRI make an all-out push to topple Saddam's regime when it was reeling after the 1991 Gulf War—despite the massacres of Iraqi Shi'a—because Tehran feared a confrontation with the victorious U.S. and other coalition forces.

The restraints states impose are often best observed in what terrorist groups do not do. As Iran sought to improve its reputation in Europe and the Middle East, the Lebanese Hizballah curtailed its attacks on targets in Europe and on Israeli targets worldwide, focusing instead on expelling Israel from the security zone along the Lebanon-Israel border: a struggle widely seen as legitimate in many parts of the world. . . .

Iran's Hesitancy to Transfer Major Weaponry to Terrorists

The picture painted thus far is not pretty, but it is not hopeless either. One bright spot is that Iran's past behavior suggests it is not likely to provide chemical, biological, radiological, or nuclear weapons to a terrorist group. Because these weapons can be devastating—or, at the very least, psychologically terrifying even when the number directly affected is low—they are far more likely to provoke escalation. In addition, these weapons are widely seen as heinous, potentially de-legitimating both the group and its state sponsor. Perhaps not surprisingly, Iran has not transferred chemical or biological weapons or agents to its proxies, despite its capability to do so.

Tehran has also sought at least a degree of deniability in its use of terrorism—a reason it often works through the Lebanese Hizballah to this day when backing terrorists. As Iran expert Kenneth Pollack notes, a chemical or biological attack (to say nothing of a nuclear strike) would lead the victim to respond with full force almost immediately. The use of proxies or cutouts would not shield Iran from retaliation.

[The 2001 terrorist attack on the World Trade Center and the Pentagon on] September 11 has also had a limiting effect. The attacks occurred over a year after the Israeli withdrawal from Lebanon. The tremendous worldwide concern about terrorism, and the active U.S. campaign against Al Qaeda, made Iran's proxies cautious about any attacks that would lead them to be compared to Al Qaeda.

Nor do Iran's favored proxies actively seek weapons of mass destruction as does Al Qaeda. They appear to recognize the "red line" drawn by the United States and other powers with regard to terrorist use of these weapons. Moreover, their current tactics and systems enable them to inflict considerable casualties. Indeed, some of the more available types of chemical and biological agents would be difficult for even a skilled terrorist group to use to inflict mass casualties, although the psychological impact would be considerable from even a limited attack with unconventional weapons.

Tehran is not likely to change its behavior on this score except in the most extreme circumstances. Traditional terrorist tactics such as assassinations and truck bombs have proven effective for Tehran. Only in the event of a truly grave threat such as an invasion of Iran would many of Tehran's traditional cautions go out the window.

> "Ahmadinejad's Holocaust denial and
> threats to 'wipe Israel off the map' rep-
> resent the ingrained ideology of [the
> Iranian clergy and the Islamic Revolu-
> tionary Guard Corps]."

Iran Is a Threat to Israel's Existence

Michael Rubin

*Israel is the United States' closest ally in the Middle East, mak-
ing Iran's anti-Semitic rhetoric and President Mahmoud
Ahmadinejad's vehement Holocaust denial particularly troubling
to many American observers. In the viewpoint that follows,
Michael Rubin expresses his concern that a nuclear-armed Iran
represents a threat to Israel's very existence. Rubin traces Iranian
anti-Semitism throughout the country's history and maintains
that the historical precedent shows a deep-seated hatred for Ju-
daism that could translate into aggression against the Jewish
state of Israel if Iran gained sufficient military strength. Rubin is
a resident scholar focusing on Middle East issues at the American Enterprise Institute for Public Policy Research, a conservative
public policy organization.*

Michael Rubin, "Iran Means What It Says," *AEI Online: On the Issues*, January 25, 2006.
Reproduced with the permission of the American Enterprise Institute for Public Policy
Research, Washington, D.C.

As you read, consider the following questions:

1. What statement, cited by Rubin, belied former so-called reformist president of Iran Mohammed Khatami's true feelings toward Israel?

2. According to the author, who was the intended audience of the 2005 "World without Zionism" conference in Iran?

3. What are some of the historical examples of anti-Semitism in Iran noted by Rubin?

The destruction of Israel is a pillar of the Islamic Republic's ideology. Soon after leading the Islamic Revolution [which overthrew then monarch Shah Mohammad Reza Pahlavi in 1979], Ayatollah Ruhollah Khomeini declared, "Every Muslim has a duty to prepare himself for battle against Israel." President Mahmoud Ahmadinejad's call for Israel to be "wiped off the map" may have shocked Europe, but his statements mark only a change in rhetorical style, not ideological substance. Ahmadinejad is not unhinged. He knows exactly what he is doing. It takes skill and sophistication to become mayor of Tehran, a city of more than 12 million, let alone president. When Ahmadinejad threatens to destroy Israel, he is deadly serious.

A Consensus to Destroy Israel Exists in Iran

When it comes to Israel, there is no difference between hardliners and reformers. While [former United Nations Secretary General] Kofi Annan honored [former Iranian President] Mohammad Khatami for his "dialogue of civilizations" idea, the reformist president's instructions to the Iranian people were less high-minded. "We should mobilize the whole Islamic World for a sharp confrontation with the Zionist regime," he told Iranian television on October 24, 2000. "If we abide by the Qur'an, all of us should mobilize to kill."

Khatami's comments were hardly the exception. Expediency Council chairman and former president Ali Akbar Hashemi Rafsanjani is often described by Western officials as a pragmatist. On December 14, 2001, he took the podium at Tehran University to deliver the Friday sermon, the official weekly policy statement of the Iranian government. In what should have been a wake-up call, Rafsanjani declared, "If one day, the Islamic world is also equipped with weapons like those that Israel possesses now, then the imperialists' strategy will reach a standstill because the use of even one nuclear bomb inside Israel will destroy everything. . . . It is not irrational to contemplate such an eventuality." U.S. and European analysts rationalized Rafsanjani's remarks, suggesting that he referred to self-defense only. Tellingly, though, many Iranian parliamentarians understood the Expediency Council chairman to mean what he said: threatening the offensive use of a nuclear weapon. Two years later, authorities displayed a Shihab-3 missile during a military parade draped with a banner reading, "Israel must be uprooted and erased from history."

Factionalism within Iran's ruling elite is not a reason to discount policy pronouncements, especially those that receive widespread media coverage within the Islamic Republic. Iranian media is state-controlled. Its broadcasts signal the imprimatur of the entire government. Iranian authorities are precise and sophisticated with messaging. Teachers and other state workers march at carefully choreographed rallies. At the October 2005 "World without Zionism" conference, banners calling for Israel's destruction were in English, not Persian. The intended audience was not only the masses in Tehran, Isfahan, and Shiraz, but rather Washington, Jerusalem, and Brussels.

The Dangers of Iran's Indoctrinated Hatred Toward Israel

Is the daily drill of Israel-damning in Iran only a tired exercise, a formalistic ceremony no longer accompanied by genuine passion or serious intent? Are the experts correct on this score? In a word: yes. Oblivious to the content of their own words, thousands of mosque- and *madrassa*-goers calling for the demise of Israel are not, for the most part, expressing a bona-fide, heartfelt hatred for the Jewish citizens or even the Jewish government of the state of Israel.

But therein lies the rub. In the end, it can often be far more dangerous *not* to mean what one is saying than to mean it—a point that may be illuminated by a brief detour into mass psychology. Fierce anger and hatred are highly intense, all-consuming emotions that subside quickly if the psyche is not to combust and collapse. Such emotions, moreover, are not only extremely intense but exceedingly unstable. . . .

For this reason, among others, genuine anger and hatred, of the kind that is really "meant" and strongly felt, are inefficient tools for creating or sustaining an atmosphere conducive to long-term persecution or mass murder. That is why the truly horrific atrocities in human history—the enslavements, the inquisitions, the terrorisms, the genocides—have been perpetrated not in hot blood but in cold: not as a result of urgent and immanent feeling but in the name of a transcendent ideology and as a result of painstaking indoctrination.

Ze'ev Maghen, "Eradicating the 'Little Satan': Why Iran Should Be Taken at Its Word," Commentary, *January 2009, p. 12.*

Anti-Semitism in Iran

Nor should Western officials dismiss Ahmadinejad's Holocaust denial simply because other Iranian officials are more polished. On December 14, 2005, four years to the day after Rafsanjani threatened a nuclear first strike against Israel, Ahmadinejad delivered a televised speech in which he called the Nazi murder of 6 million Jews a fabrication. "They have created a myth in the name of the Holocaust and consider it above God, religion, and the prophets . . . If someone were to deny the myth of the Jews' massacre, all the Zionist mouthpieces and the governments subservient to the Zionists [would] tear their larynxes and scream against the person as much as they [could]." In recent days, the Iranian government has underlined its point by announcing its intention to sponsor a Holocaust denial conference.

Ahmadinejad does not represent the Iranian public at large. Most Iranians are tolerant. Iranians pride themselves on being cosmopolitan. Most Iranians are polyglots [people who are multilingual], and Iran itself is more an empire than a nation. The Jewish community has long roots in Iran. Iranian Jews still make pilgrimages to Hamadan, a city in western Iran, to visit the tombs of Esther and Mordechai. The prophet Daniel walked through the lion's den in Susa, the ruins of which lie in the province of Khuzistan, not far from the Iraqi border. Even today, Iran boasts the second-largest Jewish community in the Middle East after Israel.

Irrational anti-Semitism has deep roots among Iran's clergy. The Nazi practice of forcing Jews to wear a yellow star had its origins in Iran, when in the ninth century an Abbasid caliph forced his Jewish subjects to wear yellow patches. Various subsequent rulers revived the practice for short periods of time. Shiite clerics long deemed any food touched by Jews to be unclean. While blood libel only took root in Iranian society after the sixteenth-century arrival of European ambassadors, as Iranian society wrestled with modernity, violent anti-

Semitism grew. Pogroms [riots against a particular group characterized by violence and destruction, originally referring to violence against Jews] wiped out the Jewish community in some towns and villages in Iranian Azerbaijan in the mid-nineteenth century. Serious pogroms also swept through Mashhad, a Shiite shrine city in northeastern Iran in which the current supreme leader, Ali Khamenei, was born and raised. It was also in Mashhad that, despite the off-cited mantra that there is no compulsion in Islam, Shiite clerics forcibly converted the remaining Jews to Islam under threat of death. Ayatollah Ruhollah Khomeini made anti-Semitic conspiracies a frequent theme of his speeches.

Ideological Support for Violence Against Israel

That most Iranians embrace religious and cultural diversity is irrelevant; the clergy and the Islamic Revolutionary Guard Corps—their ideological enforcers—wield the power. It is the stranglehold of ideologues over the Iranian state that makes a nuclear Iran so dangerous. The Revolutionary Guard Corps consolidated its power in the later years of the Khatami administration when it managed to scuttle contracts allowing Turkish and European firms to operate cell phone networks and the new Tehran airport. It is this ideological and xenophobic core which controls both Iran's nuclear industry and its missile programs. Ahmadinejad's Holocaust denial and threats to "wipe Israel off the map" represent the ingrained ideology of this group. Recent apocalyptic references by Ahmadinejad—who may just believe that he can hasten the return of the Hidden Imam, a Messianic Shiite figure, through violence and war—raise the stakes.

There is ample precedent that the Islamic Republic acts on its ideology, motivated as much by anti-Semitism as by denial of Israel's right to exist. Iranian diplomats and intelligence agents coordinated the devastating 1994 attack on the Jewish community center in Buenos Aires, Argentina. In 2002, two years after Israel's withdrawal from southern Lebanon, [Shiite terrorist organization] Hizbullah leader Hassan Nasrallah told Lebanon's *Daily Star*, "If they [the Jews] all gather in Israel, it will save us the trouble of going after them worldwide." The Islamic Republic remains Hizbullah's greatest supplier of arms and money.

> "It would take years, perhaps decades, for Iran to equal Israel's nuclear capability."

Iran Is Not a Threat to Israel's Existence

Jeremiah Haber

Israel's concern over Iran's possession of nuclear weapons is predicated on the fear that Iran would use these arms to destroy Israel. Jeremiah Haber argues in the following viewpoint that this fear is misplaced. Haber contends that Iran has never directly threatened to obliterate Israel, and he notes that Israel's weapons capabilities greatly exceed those of Iran. Haber believes that the fears of a warhead-wielding Iran are "Zionist hysteria" perpetrated by individuals with a specific political agenda. Haber, an Orthodox Jewish studies professor, teaches in both Israel and the United States.

As you read, consider the following questions:

1. Haber compares Iranian President Mahmoud Ahmadinejad's feelings about Israel to which American president's feelings about a former enemy?

Jeremiah Haber, "The Zionist Hysteria over Iran," *Catholic New Times*, May 11, 2009, p. 18. Reproduced by permission of the author.

2. What Iranian behavior does Haber see as more of a threat to Israel than its possession of nuclear weapons?

3. What does Haber believe to be the sources of "Zionist hysteria"?

I ran president Mahmoud Ahmadinejad is not my cup of tea, to say the least. I look at him and see an Iranian version of one of our Shas [a political party in Israel] politicians, and I don't like them, or their political-religious fundamentalism either. His human rights record isn't great; he is a lousy president; the Iranian people would do well to get rid of him.

No Threats of Israel's Destruction Have Come from Iran

So I am not going to defend him or make apologies for him—even though he has never threatened to destroy Israelis, and, needless to say, he has never threatened to wipe Israel off the map.

(If you don't believe me, read the wikipedia article Ahmadinejad and Israel—which is not, apparently, even disputed by the Hasbara-niks [term referring to staunch supporters of Israel] and the neo-cons.) Of course Ahmadinejad wants the State of Israel to vanish from the face of the earth. Big deal. [Ronald] Reagan wanted the same thing to happen to the Soviet Union. Most Arab states, and all Palestinians I know, see no justification for a Jewish state in Palestine.

Some are willing to make peace with it, but no Arab I know is a political Zionist (I realize that there are folks like that; the hasbara [pro-Israel] people trot them out, occasionally, or so I have been told.)

Ahmadinejad has never called for massacring Jews. As [*New York Times* journalist] Roger Cohen points out, if he is another Hitler, then why doesn't he treat his Jews the way Hitler treated German Jews? Even if life isn't a picnic for the Iranian Jewish community, they have suffered less loss of property than have Palestinian Israelis, and much less than Palestinians under the permanent Occupation [of Israelis in Palestinian territory].

Given the fact that neither Ahmadinejad's anti-Zionism nor his Holocaust denial poses any sort of threat to Israel (except in the eyes of the *Commentary* [Jewish magazine] crowd and some politicians), then the only rational grounds for Israel's sabre-rattling against Iran is Iran's support of [terrorist groups] Hezbollah and Hamas.

Zionist Hysteria

Now that makes sense. That's where Israel should be focusing its attention. And yet, when Israel and its Jewish supporters (and an occasional politician courting Jewish votes) go bonkers over Iran, it is not over its support of Palestinian and Lebanese insurgent groups, but over its nuclear program.

Will somebody explain to me why Israel has the right to have nuclear weapons but Iran, or the Arab countries do not? (Besides, of course, the rights that your tribe has over other tribes, regardless of international law and conventions.) Israel is afraid that Iran would wipe it off the map? Hasn't an Israeli minister (Fouad Ben-Eliezer, I believe) threatened Iran with that? And doesn't Iran have more to fear from Israel than vice-versa?

In fact, it would take years, perhaps decades, for Iran to equal Israel's nuclear capability. Given that Ahmadinejad has proven himself (with the help of [George W.] Bush-[Dick] Cheney) to be an astute leader in terms of Middle East power politics, given that he is no Idi Amin [military dictator and president of Uganda from 1971 to 1979] (and not even a Mu'amar Qaddafi [who assumed leadership of Libya in a 1969 coup]), given that he knows when to back off, why the cause of hysteria?

That there is Zionist hysteria cannot be denied. The affliction is particularly noticeable among the liberal hawks. Re-

Israeli Attempts to Halt Iranian Nuclear Development

Israel's intelligence service, the Mossad, has intensified its war against Iran's nuclear programme and, by some accounts, its Kidron (Bayonet) hit teams are reportedly targeting Iranian nuclear scientists for assassination as well as sabotaging the Islamic Republic's global network for procuring vital material.

Assassination is something the Mossad has carried out in the past to decapitate efforts by Israel's enemies to develop weapons of mass destruction that pose a mortal threat to the Jewish state. In the 1960s, it was Operation Damocles, repeated attacks against German scientists, some of the former Nazis, working with Egypt to build rockets armed with chemical warheads. Several Germans were assassinated by letter bombs.

In the 1980s and '90s, it was the systematic killing of key figures in Saddam's [Hussein, then president of Iraq] weapons programmes—at least three high-level scientists—and the bombing of European companies supplying components for the Iraqi dictator's secret programme to manufacture nuclear bombs. The cores for two French-built reactors bound for Iraq were blown up in a warehouse outside Toulon, France, on 5 April 1979 in Operation Sphinx.

Ed Blanche,
"Iran-Israel Covert War,"
Middle East, July 2009.

porter Daniel Luban has a great piece about [author] Jeffrey Goldberg's hysteria. It should be must reading for anybody who wants to penetrate the psyche of the species.

Israel's own liberal hawk columnist, Ari Shavit, has produced an extraordinary rant, a scare-scenario with the typical, glatt kosher Israeli message to [President Barack] Obama (tinged with the customary Israeli condescension to African Americans). The message? Stop talking about dialogue with Iran; they may not be Arabs, but they sure act like them; they only understand force. If you don't act now, it will be the *end of civilization as we know it*, or, at least, the *end of your regime*.

Sources of Israel's Insecurity

What are the sources of Shavit's hysteria? I think it has many sources: the Jewish fantasy (partly kabbalistic [dealing with mystical aspects of Judaism]) that Jews are at the center of the universe; the Iron Wall philosophy of the political Zionists [to protect Israeli settlements from the Palestinians at all costs] ([exemplified by quotes such as] "Morality is a luxury for Switzerland"; "This is the Middle East"; "We have to outbastard the bastards.") Throw in some post-Holocaust trauma for the children of the survivors, but not, of course, for the actual survivors.

And, of course, the galling fact that guys like Iran can even have a nuclear bomb. I mean, it was one thing when their film industry was doing better among international critics and festivals than Israel's. But nukes?

Anyway, Shavit's piece is worth reading for the psychological malaise that is essential to his type of Zionist. In fact, some of the other articles in *Haaretz* [a daily Israeli newspaper] on Independence Day illustrate this well. When somebody has to write an "I-am-proud-to-be-a-Zionist" piece, a century after Zionism and 61 years after the birth of the Zionist state, you know that there is still a problem. Israel has not succeeded in getting rid of the question mark over its very legitimacy. Tribalists, of course, will attribute that to the "New Antisemitism." They will forget that the legitimacy of Israel was then, as now, predicated on finding an agreed-upon solution for both the Jewish and the Palestinian peoples, and that the little matter of ethnic cleansing of 700,000 Palestinians (all "cleansed," by the way, on the same day and at the same hour—when Israel passed its Nationality Law) has come back to haunt Israel

As long as one side is not free, neither side will be free.

Periodical Bibliography

The following articles have been selected to supplement the diverse views presented in this chapter.

Kurt Andersen   "Nuclear Meltdown," *New York*, November 12, 2007.

Alastair Crooke   "The Essence of Islamist Resistance: A Different View of Iran, Hezbollah and Hamas," *NPQ: New Perspectives Quarterly*, Summer 2009.

Economist   "Spinning Dark New Tales," September 12, 2009.

Steven Erlanger   "Iran Is Still a Nuclear Threat, Israel Tells U.S. Military Chief," *New York Times*, December 11, 2007.

William F. Jasper   "No State Sponsors, No Terror," *New American*, August 31, 2009.

Stew Magnuson   "Middle East Arms Race," *National Defense*, May 2009.

Azar Nafisi   "Culture War," *New Republic*, April 23, 2007.

Grace Nasri   "Iran: Island of Stability or Land in Turmoil," *DOMES*, Spring 2009.

Jonathan Schanzer   "The Iranian Gambit in Gaza," *Commentary*, February 2009.

William Schneider   "Israel's Agenda," *National Journal*, February 22, 2009.

CHAPTER 2

How Should U.S. Foreign Policy Address Iran?

Chapter Preface

In a 2002 speech, President George W. Bush lumped Iran, North Korea, and Iraq together into a loose confederation that he dubbed the "Axis of Evil." Although these nations were not working cooperatively, Bush claimed that each represented a threat to the United States and the free world because their respective governments were supporting terrorism and seeking to acquire weapons of mass destruction. Of Iran's Tehran government, the president said, "Iran aggressively pursues [weapons of mass destruction] and exports terror, while an unelected few repress the Iranian people's hope for freedom." Because of this accusation, U.S. policy toward Iran under the Bush administration consisted of cold detachment. The U.S. government refused to negotiate with the theocratic regime, which it considered illegitimate, undemocratic, and hostile. Bush continued the decades-long practice of economic sanctions against Iran, hoping that the pressure would eventually force Iran to give up its nuclear program and encourage its people to overthrow what the United States believed to be an oppressive, clerical dictatorship.

Many European nations were upset with President Bush's pronouncement. Leaders in France, Britain, and Germany expected that diplomatic give-and-take would convince Iran to end its nuclear interests for broader economic concessions. Without U.S. involvement in this bargaining process, the plan had little hope of success. Bush vowed that America would only consider incentive packages to Iran if Tehran agreed to cease its nuclear program, and Iranian President Mahmoud Ahmadinejad made it clear that Iran would not be bullied by the United States or its European allies. With Iran's stout rebuff, Britain, France, and Germany joined Bush's cause in calling for an end to Iran's nuclear ambitions as a sign of good faith in maintaining peace in the Middle East.

When President Barack Obama took office in 2009, his administration had to decide if U.S. policy toward Iran would change from the Bush mandates. During his presidential campaign, Obama said he would be willing to sit down with Iran's leaders "without preconditions" to negotiate an end to Iran's support for terror and a curtailing of any attempt to build nuclear weapons. As president, however, his rhetoric has shifted. With Tehran's admission that it has two dormant uranium enrichment facilities, Obama has maintained that Iran would have to give up its weapons program in order to benefit from U.S. financial investment, other economic incentives, and normalized diplomatic relations. "They are going to have to make a choice: Are they willing to go down the path to greater prosperity and security for Iran, giving up the acquisition of nuclear weapons . . . or will they continue down a path that is going to lead to confrontation," Obama said in late 2009. Tehran claims its enrichment operations are designed strictly to provide nuclear power for civilian use, but European and U.S. governments are skeptical. President Obama began canvassing the international community, including the hitherto reluctant China and Russia, to wage new sanctions—the traditional U.S. policy approach—to compel Iran to prove that its nuclear agenda is confined to the peaceful production of electrical power.

In the following chapter, experts and observers debate U.S. foreign policy toward Iran, assessing its successes and failures in influencing the Tehran government. Some believe that diplomacy will resolve the tension between the two nations, while others insist that Iran's tyrannical leadership can be swayed only through tough, uncompromising confrontation.

> *"Iran will likely take no decision to halt its nuclear programme absent diplomatic contact with the United States and multilateral discussions about regional security."*

Diplomacy Would Minimize the Iranian Nuclear Threat

Andrew Parasiliti

In the viewpoint that follows, Andrew Parasiliti outlines the case for increasing U.S. diplomatic relations with Iran as a means of halting Iranian nuclear proliferation. Parasiliti examines the previous attempts at contact between the two countries and points out flaws with each engagement. Additionally, he highlights the ineffectual sanctions that have been imposed on Iran in recent years. He argues that for the United States to establish lasting stability and security in the region, it must undertake a new, comprehensive diplomatic approach that carefully considers the Iranian position, as well as that of its allies and other powers in the region, such as Israel and Saudi Arabia. Parasiliti is the ex-

Andrew Parasiliti, "Iran: Diplomacy and Deterrence," *Survival: Global Politics and Strategy*, vol. 51, October 2009, pp. 5–13. Copyright © 2009 Taylor & Francis Group, LLC. Reproduced by permission of Taylor & Francis, Ltd., http://www.tandf.co.uk/journals and the author.

ecutive director of the International Institute for Strategic Studies-US (IISS-US) and the corresponding director for the IISS-Middle East.

As you read, consider the following questions:

1. According to reports by the U.S. Government Accountability Office, how have sanctions impacted the situation with Iran?

2. As stated by the author, how did Israel respond to U.S. Secretary of State Clinton's remarks concerning U.S. missile defense programs in the region?

3. What does the second part of Parasiliti's five-pronged diplomatic approach to addressing Iran's pursuit of nuclear weapons call for?

The [President Barack] Obama administration is not ready to concede an Iranian nuclear weapon. But absent diplomatic progress, the United States may have to accept Iran as a threshold or "virtual" nuclear power. Neither sanctions nor deterrence is likely to prevent Iran from developing a nuclear-weapons capability, although deterrence might prevent the country from detonating a nuclear device or formally declaring its nuclear status. Washington [U.S. government] has so far not threatened the use of force in Iran and is wary of the potentially negative consequences for US interests and allies of a military option that is not even certain to eliminate Iran's nuclear-weapons capability. A diplomatic breakthrough, however slim the perceived possibilities, is still the best option to halt Iran's nuclear-weapons ambitions.

Failures with Diplomacy

As of summer 2009, the Obama administration was threatening to close the window on diplomacy with Iran. US Secretary of State Hillary Clinton said on 6 August 2009 that "we are under no illusions; we were under no illusions before their elections that we can get the kind of engagement we are seeking ... We're not going to keep the window open forever." The United States was expected to take stock of the situation with Iran at the G8 [Group of 8 richest countries in the world: France, Germany, Italy, Japan, the United States, the United Kingdom, Canada, and Russia] meeting accompanying the UN [United Nations] General Assembly session in late September 2009. Absent an Iranian response to an open invitation to resume multilateral talks, Washington was expected to make the case that despite its best efforts Iran had shown itself uninterested in diplomacy, meaning the time had come to consider alternative steps, such as sanctions.

The administration's frustration is understandable. Since coming to office, President Barack Obama has offered to "extend a hand" and engage in direct talks with Iran, dropping a previous US condition that Iran should first suspend all uranium-enrichment activity, as called for by five UN Security Council resolutions. In May 2009, President Obama sent a letter to Iranian Supreme Leader Ayatollah Ali Khamenei offering a framework for talks on regional security and Iran's nuclear programme.

The disputed outcome of the Iranian presidential elections increased the administration's pessimism about the prospects for negotiations with Iran. Since 12 June, Obama has balanced his commitment to diplomacy with expressions of US sympathy and support for those Iranians who protested the election results and who have suffered imprisonment, beatings, torture, show trials, and a crackdown on media and free expression.

Obama's diplomatic initiatives have taken place in the context of failed multilateral diplomacy over Iran's nuclear programme and a well documented record of Iranian refusals to cooperate fully with the efforts of the International Atomic Energy Agency (IAEA) to verify the peaceful nature of its nuclear programmes, and to implement the IAEA Additional

Protocol. Iran has also refused to take up formal proposals from the P5+1 ([the five permanent members of the UN Security Council plus Germany] the United States, United Kingdom, Russia, China, France and Germany, as well as the European Union), which have included discussions with Iran about regional security; normalisation of political, economic, trade and energy relations; assistance with Iran's civil nuclear programme; and other incentives. Iran, in return, would suspend enrichment and reprocessing activities and cooperate fully with the IAEA. A more recent suggestion of a "double freeze" would require Iran to freeze enrichment at current levels, rather than completely suspend enrichment as called for in UN Security Council resolutions, in return for a freeze on imposition of further sanctions. Iran has yet to respond to these proposals in any meaningful way.

The U.S. Response to Continued Iranian Inaction

The diplomatic efforts of the Obama administration have been complemented by increasing "pressure" on Iran, which has been threatened with economic sanctions and warned to respond to US diplomatic overtures according to specific timelines. On 22 April 2009, Secretary of State Clinton spoke of "crippling sanctions" on Iran should the diplomatic track falter. President Obama said on 18 May 2009, at a press conference with Israeli Prime Minister Benjamin Netanyahu, that the "end of the year" would be the time to evaluate progress with Iran.

There may be several influences on the US timelines, in addition to the lack of a serious Iranian response. The 2007 National Intelligence Estimate (NIE) on Iran judged "with moderate confidence" that Iran would have the capability to produce enough highly enriched uranium (HEU) for a nuclear weapon within the "2010–2015 time frame", although "all agencies recognize the possibility that this capability may not be attained until *after* 2015." On 9 July 2009, Admiral Mike Mullen, US chairman of the Joint Chiefs of Staff, estimated that Iran could develop a nuclear-weapons capability in "one to three years." Democratic leaders in the US Congress have supported Obama's diplomatic outreach to Iran but have made clear that engagement cannot be open-ended. Meanwhile, Israel's sense of urgency about Iran's nuclear programmes is even greater than that of the United States.

The administration is threatening to move ahead with sanctions on Iran's importation and development of refined petroleum products, as well as tougher measures against Iranian financial institutions. Obama touted sanctions on Iran as a senator and candidate for president, telling the American Israeli Public Affairs Committee (AIPAC) in June 2008 that "we should work with Europe, Japan and the Gulf states to find every avenue outside the UN to isolate the Iranian regime— from cutting off loan guarantees and expanding financial sanctions, to banning the export of refined petroleum to Iran, to boycotting firms associated with the Iranian Revolutionary Guard, whose Quds force has rightly been labeled a terrorist organization." The Iran Refined Petroleum Sanctions Act so far has 72 co-sponsors in the US Senate and 294 co-sponsors in the House of Representatives.

Sanctions Have Been Ineffective

The international prospects for more sanctions on Iran are less assured than they may be in the US Congress. Russia and China support UN Security Council resolutions dealing with Iran's nuclear programme, but have as yet shown no interest in more sanctions on Iran. Both countries have their own commercial and energy relationships with Iran, and neither Moscow [Russian government] nor Beijing [Chinese government] shares US and European concerns about the disputed re-election of Iranian President Mahmoud Ahmadinejad.

All this raises a broader question about the effectiveness of pressure, timelines and sanctions in influencing Iran. The 2007 NIE assessed that Iran's decision to halt its nuclear-weapons programme in autumn 2003 was "in response to international pressure." While international sanctions on Iran may have hurt the country's economy, including the development of its energy infrastructure, they have so far not proved a deterrent to Iran's nuclear ambitions. The US Government Accountability Office (GAO) reported that "UN sanctions may also play an important role in pressuring Iran, but these sanctions have not yet been fully implemented." The GAO concluded that "the overall impact of sanctions, and the extent to which these sanctions further U.S. objectives, is unclear."

A Nuclear Iran Would Increase U.S. Involvement in the Region

The Obama administration is seeking to convince Iran that its pursuit of a nuclear weapon will be a catalyst for expanded US security relationships and commitments in the Middle East, and theatre missile defence in Europe and the Gulf. These policies are designed both to deter Iran's development of a nuclear weapon and, it seems, to prepare for a new regional security structure should Iran attain a nuclear-weapons capability.

On 7 July 2009 Admiral Mullen said that the United States was working with its Gulf partners to develop and expand "regional defense capability." That same day, President Obama linked US missile defence in Europe to a US deterrent posture toward Iran, saying,

> I've made it clear that this system is directed at preventing a potential attack from Iran. It has nothing to do with Russia . . . If the threat from Iran's nuclear and ballistic missile program is eliminated, the driving force for missile defense in Europe will be eliminated, and that is in our mutual interests.

Picking up Mullen's theme, Secretary of State Clinton said on 22 July 2009 that,

> if the United States extends a defense umbrella over the region, if we do even more to support the military capacity of those in the Gulf, it's unlikely that Iran will be any stronger or safer, because they won't be able to intimidate or dominate, as they apparently believe they can, once they have a nuclear weapon.

Consideration of U.S. Allies' Fears

While Mullen's remark passed without scrutiny, Clinton's statement caused alarm in Israel, which worried that the United States may be conceding the possibility of an Iranian nuclear weapon. US National Security Adviser James Jones led a US team to Israel the week following Clinton's remarks to assure Israeli leaders that Washington was conceding no such thing, and to brief Israel on US strategy, including sanctions on Iran.

Israel has refused to rule out the possible use of military force to prevent an Iranian nuclear weapon—an option the United States has so far sought to avoid. Washington has counselled Israeli patience and restraint in support of US policy toward Iran. But Israel's patience may have its limits, especially if Israel believes the United States may be willing to live with an Iranian nuclear weapon.

On 5 July 2009, US Vice President Joseph Biden, in response to a question about how the United States would respond to a possible Israeli military attack on Iran, said that the United States "cannot dictate to another sovereign nation what they can and cannot do when they make a determination, if they make a determination that they're existentially threatened and their survival is threatened by another country." After meeting with US Secretary of Defense Robert Gates in Israel on 27 July 2009, Prime Minister Netanyahu's office released a statement reiterating the seriousness with which Is-

Only Bilateral Communication Will Effect Change

A US decision on a new strategy toward Iran will not wait. That is President-elect [Barack] Obama's inheritance. Talking to Iran will be difficult. In the US, some political leaders and interest groups oppose better relations, though public opinion surveys suggest that a solid majority of Americans favor a diplomatic solution to US-Iranian differences over nuclear enrichment and other issues. Similarly, in Iran, an attempt to engage or compromise with the US will be attacked by factions seeking a political advantage, despite the hopes of millions of Iranians that the US and Iran find a way to improve relations. Suspicion dominates a relationship with a long history of grievances on both sides. Washington [U.S. government] doubts the innocence of Iran's nuclear intentions, and Tehran [Iranian government] suspects that America's real intent is regime change. . . .

The US can impose costs on Iran, but it cannot impose its will. The same is true for Iran. Progress requires on both sides a greater focus on strategy rather than tactics. Adopting a new, integrated approach will require political leadership that is disciplined and willing to take risks. There could be frustrations, setbacks and dangers, but the US and Iran can avoid a downward spiral that risks military conflict. They can also create an opportunity for progress on some of the most difficult and complicated challenges the US will have to confront in the coming years.

William Luers, Thomas R. Pickering, and Jim Walsh,
"How to Deal with Iran," New York Review of Books,
February 12, 2009.

rael views Iran's nuclear ambitions and "the need to utilize all available means to prevent Iran from achieving a nuclear weapons capability."

The prospect of a nuclear Iran has caused unease among US allies throughout the Middle East, who are looking for US leadership to manage that possible outcome. To address allies' concerns and demonstrate leadership in the region, conversations about a regional defence capability or defence umbrella in the Gulf are appropriate and should continue, but quietly, and in the context of a renewed and increasingly urgent diplomatic strategy.

The Necessity of U.S. Diplomatic Outreach

President Obama has been unequivocal in his commitment to preventing an Iranian nuclear weapon, but time is not on the US side. Sanctions and an emerging deterrent strategy may convey to Iran the costs of not complying with UN Security Council resolutions, and may prevent a declared nuclear weapon, although probably not a threshold or undeclared nuclear-weapons capability. Sanctions and deterrence alone are therefore unlikely to halt Iran's nuclear-weapons ambitions, encourage Israeli restraint or discourage Arab countries from pursuing their own nuclear deterrent options. The use of military force might buy time, but could also produce the consequences of a more unified and radicalised Iran, asymmetrical Iranian retaliation, or an (albeit delayed) Iranian nuclear weapon.

Iran will likely take no decision to halt its nuclear programme absent diplomatic contact with the United States and multilateral discussions about regional security. Washington should neither chase nor pressure Iran publicly, but should consider five diplomatic options, which are not mutually exclusive, while simultaneously pursuing other deterrent strategies.

A Five-Pronged Diplomatic Approach

Firstly, the United States should seek a discreet back-channel to Iran. There is a line of argument that Iran has discounted the P5+1 process because it prefers direct negotiations with the United States, and that should such negotiations occur, Iran's nuclear programme would be subsumed under discussions of regional security. This approach would allow Iran not to be perceived as being pressured into responding to US initiatives. Some cite the "Roadmap" memo drafted in 2003 by then Swiss Ambassador to Iran Tim Guldimann and Iranian Ambassador to France Sadeq Kharrazi as illustrative of a template for US-Iranian discussions, and of a now by-the-board attempt by Iran to reach out to Washington.

Secondly, given that the P5+1 forum is unlikely to be effective in engaging Iran, creative new diplomatic options need to be considered. A UN conference or forum on regional security in the Gulf, as called for in UN Security Council Resolution 598 (1987), would be a start. There may be some initial resistance by Iran and some of the other regional powers, but a suitably broad agenda, with much input by Iran, Saudi Arabia and the Gulf states, should help to overcome this. It would need to be understood, however, that the first item of business would be nuclear proliferation in the Gulf—implying Iran's nuclear programme, and that Iran, as a confidence-building step, would agree to resume full cooperation with the IAEA.

A third and related option would be for the United States to consider employing an envoy, such as UN Secretary-General Ban Ki Moon or another international statesman, to quietly begin a process of mediation.

A fourth option is progress in US-Israel-Syria relations. An improvement in ties with Syria could, over time, weaken Tehran's [the Iranian government] links to [terrorist groups] Hizbullah and Hamas and undermine Iran's position in the region.

Fifth and finally, there is a role for public diplomacy that recognises the potential for change in Iran. President Obama's speeches and remarks since 12 June have contained the right mixture of realism and principle. He should consider another major speech addressing Iran. This should be expansive and positive, reiterating US support for Iran's right to civil nuclear power as a signatory to the Non-Proliferation Treaty, engagement on regional security, and, over time, if Iran abides by UN Security Council resolutions and works transparently with the IAEA, an end to sanctions and diplomatic isolation. Obama's public-diplomacy initiative would not be about playing politics or manipulating factions inside Iran, and should not include stark warnings about pressures or timelines for diplomacy. The United States should continue to take the high ground, seeking to tap into a constituency for change among Iran's leaders and people about the direction of their country. That constituency is very much alive in Iran, and needs to be recognised, while giving continued top priority to preventing an Iranian nuclear weapon.

> *"The only consequence of engaging such a vociferously hostile regime in negotiations is the whitewashing of its crimes and the granting of undeserved legitimacy."*

Diplomacy Has Not and Will Not Minimize the Iranian Nuclear Threat

Part I: Elan Journo, Part II: Herbert I. London

In the two-part viewpoint that follows, the authors examine the historical and potential future consequences of engaging in diplomatic relations with Iran. In Part I, Elan Journo chides European diplomats for their failed negotiations with Iran in 2006. Journo argues that these talks were doomed to failure from the outset due to the nature of the Iranian regime. Further, he contends that not only did the diplomatic advances fail to curtail the Iranian nuclear program, but in fact they had the opposite effect, emboldening the Iranian regime to continue nuclear development. Herbert I. London argues in Part II that Iran will not be governed by deterrence, which limited the Soviet Union's

Part I: Elan Journo, "Why 'Diplomacy' with Iran Had to Fail," *Capitalism Magazine*, February 6, 2006. Reproduced by permission.; Part II: Herbert I. London, "Diplomacy and Deterrence Will Not Stop Iran," Townhall.com, September 25, 2008. Reproduced by permission.

use of nuclear weapons, and no amount of diplomatic advances will restrain Iranian nuclear ambitions. Possession of a nuclear weapon, London maintains, is the only means of ensured survival for the current Iranian regime, and it will pursue survival at any cost. Journo is a resident fellow focusing on foreign policy issues at the Ayn Rand Center for Individual Rights. He is the editor of the book Winning the Unwinnable War: America's Self-Crippled Response to Islamic Totalitarianism. *London is the president of the Hudson Institute, a public policy think tank, and a regular contributor to numerous major newspapers and journals.*

As you read, consider the following questions:

1. As stated by Elan Journo, what have the West's attempts at diplomatic engagement with Iran taught Iran's mullahs?

2. What does Journo say are the consequences of engaging with Iran?

3. To what historical failed diplomatic advances does Journo equate the outcome of further diplomatic attempts with Iran?

Part I

European diplomats, who courted Iran in an attempt to halt its suspected nuclear weapons program, regret that "diplomacy" did not dissuade Iran from its plans. But this failure was foreseeable.

Europe's diplomatic effort was touted as a reasonable way to settle the dispute over Iran's suspected nuclear weapons program without any losers. By enticing Iran to the negotiating table, we were told, the West can avoid a military confrontation, while Iran gains "economic incentives" that can help build its economy. But the negotiations—backed also by the [George W.] Bush administration—only strengthened Iran and turned it into a greater menace.

The proposed deal—which was said to include the sale of civilian aircraft and membership for Iran in the World Trade Organization—rested on the notion that no one would put abstract goals or principles ahead of gaining a steady flow of economic loot. And so, if only we could have negotiated a deal that gave Iran a sufficiently juicy carrot, it would forgo its ambitions.

Iran Desires Nuclear Weapons

But to believe that Iran really hungers for nuclear energy (as it claims) is sheer fantasy. Possessing abundant oil and gas reserves, Iran is the second-largest oil producer in OPEC [Organization of Petroleum Exporting Countries]. To believe that it values prosperity at all is equally fantastic; Iran is a theocracy [a government where God, in this case Allah of Islam, is seen as the supreme leader] that systematically violates its citizens' right to political and economic liberty.

What Iran desires is a nuclear weapon—the better to threaten and annihilate the impious in the West and in Iran's neighborhood. Iran declares its anti-Western ambitions stridently. At an official parade in 2004, Iran flaunted a missile draped with a banner declaring that: "We will crush America under our feet." (Its leaders, moreover, have for years repeated the demand that "Israel must be wiped off the map.")

A committed enemy of the West, Iran is the ideological wellspring of Islamic terrorism, and the "world's most active sponsor of terrorism" (according to the U.S. government). A totalitarian regime that viciously punishes "un-Islamic" behavior among its own citizens, Iran actively exports its contempt for freedom and human life throughout the infidel world. For years it has been fomenting and underwriting savage attacks on Western and American interests, using such proxies as [the terrorist group] Hezbollah. Like several of the 9/11 hijackers [who attacked the U.S. in 2001] before them, many senior al-Qaida leaders, fugitives of the Afghanistan war, have found refuge in Iran. And lately Iran has funneled millions of dollars, arms and ammunition to insurgents in Iraq.

It's absurd to think that by offering Iran rewards to halt its aggression, we will deflect it from its goal.

Diplomacy Emboldens Iran

The only consequence of engaging such a vociferously hostile regime in negotiations is the whitewashing of its crimes and the granting of undeserved legitimacy. The attempt to conciliate Iran has further inflamed the boldness of Iran's mullahs [Islamic clergy]. What it has taught them is that the West lacks the intellectual self-confidence to name its enemies and deal with them accordingly. It has vindicated the mullahs' view that their religious worldview can bring a scientific, technologically advanced West to its knees.

Whether or not negotiations yield a deal, "diplomacy" abets Iran. The deal would have sustained Iran's economy, propped up its dictatorial government and perpetuated its terrorist war against the West. But even without a deal, simply by prolonging "negotiations," Iran grows stronger because it gains time to continue covert nuclear-weapons research.

Previous Diplomatic Failures

This approach of diplomacy-with-anyone-at-any-cost necessarily results in nourishing one's enemy and sharpening its fangs. That is what happened under a 1994 deal with communist North Korea. After endless negotiations and offers of aid, North Korea promised not to develop nuclear weapons. When the North was caught cheating on its pledge, the West pursued yet more negotiations, and the North eventually promised anew to end its nuclear program. In February 2005 North Korea declared (plausibly) that it had succeeded in building nuclear weapons.

Another, older, attempt to negotiate with an avowed enemy was a cataclysmic failure. In 1938 the Europeans pretended that [Adolf] Hitler's intentions were not really hostile, and insisted that "peace in our time" could be brokered diplomatically (by letting him take Czechoslovakia). The negotiations afforded him time to build his military machine and emboldened him to launch World War II.

Ignoring the lessons of history, the Europeans embarked on negotiations with Iran that likewise sought the reckless pretence of peace today, at the cost of unleashing catastrophic dangers tomorrow.

To protect American (and European) lives, we must learn the life-or-death importance of passing objective moral judgment. By any rational standard, Iran should be condemned and its nuclear ambition thwarted, now. The brazenly amoral European gambit has only aided its quest—and will entail a future confrontation with a bolder, stronger Iran.

Part II

For the sake of American security it is critical to understand the consequences of a nuclear Iran, because the current approach of sanctions and diplomacy will ultimately fail in preventing the development of the nuclear weapons Iran sees as its ticket to regional hegemony.

A Nuclear Iran Will Not Be Deterred

The belief that if Iran obtains nuclear weapons it can be deterred, just as the Soviet Union was deterred during the Cold War, is neither safe nor responsible. The Soviet Union was deterred largely because its finances could no longer support its vast empire in an arms race. Iran however, holds claim to the world's third largest oil reserves, which in today's environment provides them considerable economic power.

The more logical comparison of Iran's potential power would be the former ambitions of Iraq under Saddam Hussein. If Iraq had had the patience to wait to develop nuclear weapons before it invaded Kuwait [as it did in August 1990, sparking the Persian Gulf War, in which the United States and its allies ultimately prevailed], the history of the last 20 years in the Persian Gulf would look very different. Confronted with a choice of having Iraq in possession of the Kuwait and Saudi oilfields, versus going to war with a nuclear power—what would the world have chosen?

As Arthur Borden outlined in his excellent recent book *A Better Country*, the threat Iraq would have posed if armed with nuclear weapons, combined with its aggressive tendencies was the real reason America invaded Iraq. As Borden explains, this has been America's Middle Eastern policy dating back to President [Jimmy] Carter's 1980 State of the Union address, when he stated: "An attempt by any outside force to gain control of the Persian Gulf region will be regarded as an assault on the vital interests of the United States of America, and such an assault will be repelled by any means necessary, including military force." A nuclear-armed Iran will eviscerate that policy.

Moreover, Iran can derive these benefits without even producing a weapon. All it has to do is get close by enriching enough uranium to produce a bomb, maintaining a warhead development program and securing delivery capability.

Limits of U.S. Diplomacy

Diplomacy cannot halt this gathering threat. Is the U.S., for example, inoculated against a grand bargain in which Iran's regional dominance is acknowledged in return for non-deployment of nuclear weapons? A concession Iran could achieve without actually possessing an actual bomb. Cheering on the sidelines would be Russia and China eager to diminish United States' influence in the Middle East and eager as well to either obtain oil for a growing economy as is the case with China or maintain high oil prices which benefit the relatively oil rich Russian economy.

These weapons would also undermine the non-proliferation treaty and the role of the U.N. [United Nations] as an arbiter for stability, a role it has tended to exercise in the breach in any case. By thumbing its nose at the world, Iran can become a regional and arguably a world power capable of advancing its own agenda.

Last, rather than deter an enemy which is the presumption behind evolving State Department logic, the administration will be deterred from actions. It is apparent in the five party talks with North Korea that the U.S. has very little leverage other than acting as a supplicant offering a carrot and yet another carrot to a rogue state with nuclear weapons.

Any way one looks at it, the U.S. would be bargaining from a position of weakness even if the mullahs relying on theological considerations were willing to bargain at all. After all, nuclear weapons represent an insurance policy for the survival of the regime and regional hegemony.

In the case that Iran truly ceased its nuclear weapons program in 2003 as the National Intelligence Estimate [NIE] report asserts, it probably did not do so because of negotiation, another NIE assertion, but rather because of the American invasion of Iraq in that year. If we triumph in Iraq only to allow Iran to progress towards their goal of regional power unfettered then the entire effort will have been in vain.

> *"Tehran is likely to end its problematic actions only if it is convinced that failing to do so would bring consequences that threaten its own hold on power."*

The United States Should Impose Harsher Sanctions on Iran

James Phillips

The United States has often imposed sanctions on countries that it deems a substantial threat to international peace and global security. In the case of Iran, the U.S. government has limited exports and restricted international investment in the Iranian economy. James Phillips argues in the following viewpoint that in light of Iran's continued support of terrorism, secretive nuclear development, and human rights abuses, the United States should levy harsher sanctions to exert greater pressure on the governing regime to cease these objectionable actions. Phillips believes that the Iranian government will be particularly vulnerable to increased international economic pressure due to growing political unrest in the country as well as high unemployment and inflation rates. Considering the current state of upheaval in Iran,

Phillips believes that the regime will be more likely to change its behavior in response to tougher sanctions that could amplify the instability there. Phillips is a senior research fellow for Middle Eastern affairs at the Heritage Foundation.

As you read, consider the following questions:

1. What penalties would the proposed Iran Refined Petroleum Sanctions Act place on Iran if Congress passes this legislation, according to Phillips?

2. What are the unemployment and inflation rates in Iran, as reported by the author?

3. What does Phillips claim to be "even more important than new U.S. sanctions" in exerting pressure on the Iranian regime?

There is growing bipartisan momentum in Congress to impose further sanctions on Iran. This long-overdue action, which would strengthen U.S. diplomatic leverage over Tehran [the capital of Iran], should be welcomed by the [Barack] Obama Administration and integrated into its dual-track strategy for Iran.

New sanctions or measures to tighten up existing sanctions would send a strong signal to Iran's Islamist dictatorship that its support for terrorism, duplicity on its nuclear program, and widespread human rights abuses will trigger increasingly severe repercussions. Tehran is likely to end its problematic actions only if it is convinced that failing to do so would bring consequences that threaten its own hold on power.

Iran's Continued Hostility and Violence

Iran ranks as the world's foremost state sponsor of terrorism and supports hostile groups in Iraq and Afghanistan that target American soldiers on a daily basis. The radical Islamist regime poses a threat not only to the United States and its allies but to the Iranian people, which it continues to brutally repress after crushing a popular opposition movement that was galvanized by President Mahmoud Ahmadinejad's widely disputed "re-election" last June [2009].

Iran continues to hold as hostages three American hikers and two American citizens of Iranian descent and is suspected of involvement in the disappearance of retired FBI [Federal Bureau of Investigation] investigator Robert Levinson in Iran in 2007. But for many in Congress, the last straw was the September 24 [2009] revelation by President Obama that Western intelligence agencies had discovered a uranium enrichment facility that Iran had tried to hide for several years.

Plans for Gasoline Import Sanctions

On September 26, the chairman of the House Foreign Affairs Committee, Howard Berman (D-CA), announced that he will fast-track Iran sanctions legislation in his committee. Berman said that the committee will soon consider the Iran Refined Petroleum Sanctions Act, which he had introduced along with Representative Ileana Ros-Lehtinen (R-FL), the ranking Republican on the committee.

This promising bill would increase the size of financial penalties against Iran and bar a handful of foreign companies that sell gasoline and other refined petroleum products to Iran from doing business in the United States. Iran is vulnerable to a cut-off of gasoline imports, which provide up to 40 percent of its consumption. The regime's attempts to reduce this vulnerability through rationing triggered riots in 2007 and remain a sore point with Iran's citizens today.

Three original sponsors of the Senate version of the Iran Refined Petroleum Sanctions Act, Senators Jon Kyl (R-AZ), Joseph Lieberman (I-CT), and Evan Bayh (D-IN), called on September 25 for the urgent passage of the bill, which has attracted 76 co-sponsors. The three issued a joint statement:

The Impact of Banking Sanctions on Iran

From the vantage point of Iranian businesspeople seeking a friction-free financial relationship with the outside world, the costs of financial pressure have been high and unwelcome. Costs associated with Iranian trade have reportedly gone up by between 10 and 30 percent. The vice president of the Dubai-based Iranian Business Council has stated that no one is accepting Iranian letters of credit anymore, which is why Iranians are moving out of Iran in order to establish relationships with other foreign banks. In June [2008], *The Washington Post* reported that the honorary president of the private German-Iranian Chamber of Commerce said that the financial sanctions against Iran's international banking network have made it nearly impossible to pay for goods.

The banking squeeze has also put a hold on foreign investment. Chinese banks reportedly have scaled back ties with Iranian companies at a time when Iran is looking to China as part of its great reorientation eastward. This is to say nothing of the numerous oil and gas deals that have hobbled along erratically as companies and their banks retreat from doing business with Iran. According to the UN [United Nations] Conference on Trade and Developments 2007 World Investment Report, Iran kept company with Iraq, Kuwait, the Palestinian territories, Syria, and Yemen in attracting the lowest levels of foreign investment in the Middle East.

Rachel L. Loeffler,
"Bank Shots," Foreign Affairs,
March–April 2009.

"Given Iran's consistent pattern of deceit, concealment, and bad faith, the only way to force Iran to abandon its nuclear ambitions is to make absolutely clear to the regime in Tehran that its current course will carry catastrophic consequences. We must leave no doubt that we are prepared to do whatever it takes to stop Iran's nuclear breakout."

This week [in October 2009], Senate Banking Committee Chairman Christopher Dodd indicated that he will introduce legislation that will incorporate the Senate version of the Iran Refined Petroleum Sanctions Act along with other sanctions such as tougher export controls and enhanced authority for freezing the assets of Iranian entities that support terrorism or proliferation activities.

The Obama Administration is also reportedly scrambling to put together a package of sanctions after the latest revelations about Iran's nuclear deceptions. But some within and outside the Administration are likely to argue that sanctions should be kept on hold as long as the P5+1 [the five permanent members of the United Nations Security Council: France, the United Kingdom, the United States, China and Russia, plus Germany] talks continue.

This is the wrong approach, because it gives Tehran every incentive to prolong the talks and stave off sanctions without fully complying with repeated U.N. [United Nations] Security Council resolutions demanding that it freeze its uranium enrichment activities. There is no time to waste, given that Iran already has the knowledge, technological infrastructure, and growing stocks of refined uranium to build a bomb in the coming months.

Iran's Vulnerability to Sanctions

The decline in the global price of oil, which provides about 80 percent of Iran's export revenues, has left Tehran more vulnerable to foreign economic pressures. The fall of oil prices from their 2008 peak, growing domestic consumption of oil, and problems in maintaining the volume of Iran's oil exports have led to a sharp decline in Iran's oil export revenues, which has exacerbated structural weaknesses in the Iranian economy.

Sanctions levied now are likely to have more political impact within Iran than in the past, given the growing opposition to the regime, an unemployment rate of over 20 percent, and an annual inflation rate of about 13 percent.

Even more important than new U.S. sanctions would be greater international participation in existing sanctions on Iranian banks, the Revolutionary Guards, and other entities that support terrorism, Iran's military buildup, and its nuclear program. Especially needed are the adoption and implementation of stronger export controls by our allies—particularly in Europe—to restrict the export of nuclear, military, and dual-use technologies to Iran. Broadening international participation in tightening existing sanctions on Iran is also important, because Russia and China are likely to delay and dilute any new sanctions at the U.N. Security Council.

Sanctions alone are unlikely to be decisive in changing Iranian behavior, but they can substantially raise the economic, political, and diplomatic costs to the regime of continuing its current hostile policies and drive a deeper wedge between the regime and the Iranian people. For sanctions to work, there must be widespread international cooperation in enforcing them over a prolonged period of time. But Iran may be only months away from attaining a nuclear weapon.

The sooner Congress acts on sanctions, the better. However, only decisive leadership from President Obama, supported by a broad international coalition willing to enforce much more harsh sanctions and backed by the credible threat of military force, is ultimately likely to force Tehran to give up its nuclear ambitions.

> *"Proponents of sanctions need to prove that sanctions were responsible for the weak [Iranian] economy in 2008."*

The United States Should Not Impose Harsher Sanctions on Iran

Djavad Salehi-Isfahani

Over the past 30 years, the United States has imposed numerous sanctions on Iran. Proponents of these measures contend that the sanctions have caused Iran's current state of economic and political upheaval, and that now is the time to implement increasingly harsh economic penalties to end the current regime's objectionable behavior. In the following viewpoint, however, Djavad Salehi-Isfahani argues that these assumptions about the impact of the sanctions are wrong. He contends that there is no proof of a causal relationship between the sanctions and Iran's current political discontent and economic downturn. He warns that increasing U.S. sanctions against the country could further cement the current leadership's position of power instead of influencing its behavior or causing its ultimate downfall. A professor of eco-

Djavad Salehi-Isfahani, "Iran Sanctions: Who Really Wins?" *Brookings*, September 30, 2009. Reproduced by permission.

nomics at Virginia Tech, Salehi-Isfahani spent a year at Harvard University as a Dubai Initiative research fellow at the Belfer Center for Science and International Affairs.

As you read, consider the following questions:

1. What two assumptions used to support increasing sanctions on Iran does Salehi-Isfahani find questionable?

2. As stated by the author, what were the "most crippling blows" to the Iranian economy?

3. When, according to the author, are sanctions as a tool for foreign policy most effective, and does he believe Iran is experiencing these conditions?

U.S. and Iranian representatives meet this week [September 2009] at a time when trust between the two countries is at a low ebb following the revelation last week of a previously undisclosed Iranian nuclear facility under construction and the test firing of Iran's long-range missiles on September 28. Meanwhile, the [President Barack] Obama administration's policy of engagement with Iran has emerged as little more than the old policy of "carrots and sticks."

The focus of the debate in the U.S. has shifted from Iran's internal political crisis to its economy. The group of 5+1 (the five UN [United Nations] Security Council members [China, France, Russia, the United Kingdom, and the United States] plus Germany) is weighing the costs and benefits of additional sanctions on Iran as a way of pressuring the [President Mahmoud] Ahmadinejad government to change its position on the nuclear issue.

The discussion on sanctions takes place under considerable uncertainty about their effectiveness and the state of Iran's economy. The emerging consensus in Washington [D.C.] that new, "crippling" sanctions could persuade Iran to change its nuclear policy seems in part based on the lack of a better alternative. But it is also based on two assumptions that I find questionable: first, that the existing sanctions are largely responsible for the weak state of Iran's economy and second, that the weak economy has helped fuel the popular discontent that boiled over in [capital of Iran] Tehran's streets this summer.

The Missing Link Between Sanctions and Iran's Poor Economy

The premise of the first assumption—Iran's weak economy—was revealed last week to be truer than most people (including myself) had anticipated. Survey data released by the Statistical Center of Iran indicate that the performance of the economy last year was the worst in recent memory. Last year incomes fell by a whopping 20 percent in rural areas and 10 percent in urban areas. Such annual declines in consumer incomes have not been seen before, even during the worst years of the Iran-Iraq war. Confirmation that the economy did actually shrink must await the publication of the national accounts for last year by the Central Bank, which has delayed their release. These figures are unlikely to change the bleak picture painted by the survey data, because private consumption accounts for about 55 percent of Gross Domestic Expenditures (GDE) and investment, which accounts for another third of the GDE, likely took a similar hit. Investment was probably the first to drop, as the private sector lost confidence in government policy and the public sector diverted its own investment funds to pay for its populist programs.

Proponents of sanctions need to prove that sanctions were responsible for the weak economy in 2008. This is difficult to do, because the same sanctions were in effect in 2007 when the economy enjoyed a robust growth rate of about 7 percent. True, the sanctions may have taken time to bite, but the government's own policies are a major source of Iran's economic woes. A case in point is the banking crisis in Iran which contributed to the economic downturn in 2008. In principle, this crisis could be attributed to sanctions that prohibited U.S. and participating banks in other countries from doing business with Iranian banks which, in effect, severely disrupted financial flows that connected Iran to the outside world and scared off private investment. However, the most crippling blows actually came from inside Iran. The Ahmadinejad government lowered interest rates by fiat [authoritative decree] and, as a cornerstone of its redistributive policies, at the same time pushed for a massive expansion of credit to small and medium sized enterprises, forcing banks to lend at interest rates 5 to 10 percent below the rate of inflation. In an attempt to restrain the expansion of bank credit and the resulting inflation, the Central Bank stepped in and effectively stopped the program. Ahmadinejad dismissed two central bank governors, but tight money prevailed and inflation dropped sharply, from 25 percent in 2008 to the current annual rate of about 15 percent. The cost has been the present deep recession.

Misreading Cause and Effect in Iran

The problem with the argument that sanctions have inflicted damage to the Iranian economy goes beyond a problem in attribution of cause and effect and to simple misreading of data on Iran's economy. Descriptions of the economy as "dilapidated" or "teetering" are misleading, because Iran's economy has been on a growth trajectory for the past decade. Over this time, it has doubled per capita incomes, expanded basic services like water and electricity to over 95 percent of the population, and helped expand the country's systems of health care and education, which are the envy of its neighbors. Even as the economy was in serious decline last year, the proportion of urban Iranian households with a cell phone jumped from 64 to 79 percent (from 31 to 50 percent for rural households).

Hurdles to Effective Sanctions in Iran

Since the 1979 Islamic Revolution [in which the Shah's monarchy was overthrown and replaced by the theocratic Islamic Republic of Iran], the United States has imposed different types of economic sanctions on Iran. After long and complicated negotiations, the United Nations Security Council unanimously adopted Resolution 1737 in December 2006. The resolution imposed sanctions that targeted ten Iranian organizations or companies and twelve individuals associated with [Iranian capital] Tehran's nuclear and ballistic missile programs. In September 2006, the United States banned dollar transactions with Bank Saderat, Iran's largest commercial bank. And in January 2007, the U.S. Treasury imposed sanctions against Sepah, Iran's oldest bank. Economic sanctions, however, have to overcome two main hurdles. Given Iran's substantial hydrocarbon resources and its large population (approximately seventy million), several European and Asian countries see Iran as an attractive trade and financial partner. Furthermore, economic sanctions could hurt ordinary Iranians, the same people whose support Washington [D.C.] says it seeks against "the ruling elite."

Gawdat Bahgat, "Iran and the United States: Reconcilable Differences," Iranian Studies, April 2008.

It is a further misreading of Iran to believe, as many proponents of sanctions do, that the tensions that boiled over into Tehran's streets this summer were proof of mass dissatisfaction with rising poverty and economic stagnation. The sharp economic decline in 2008 no doubt contributed to dis-

satisfaction, but for the most part what was on display in Tehran after the disputed election was more the fruits of improvements in living standards than economic decline. The
economic growth of the last decade, boosted by effective health
and education policies since the Islamic Revolution [1979],
has doubled the size of the middle class and reduced the
ranks of the poor by two-thirds. Sanctions that reverse these
trends may hurt rather than help the cause of moderation in
Iran. These considerations lead to a different view of sanctions.

Sanctions Could Increase Support for President Ahmadinejad

The case for sanctions as an effective foreign policy tool is
strongest when the country in question is brimming with internal political tensions caused by years of stagnation or decline in living standards, which sanctions can intensify to
bring about the desired policy shift by the country's rulers.
This is not the situation in Iran.

The sizeable majority of Iran's economically disadvantaged
population that supports the Ahmadinejad government is not
poor in the sense of lacking food and shelter. Its support for
the current government signifies a clear choice between a
populist leader with oil money to distribute and his liberal
opponents, who criticize his redistributive policies for being
inflationary and dismiss them as mere charity. In this political
atmosphere sanctions are likely to cement the authoritarian
pact between the conservatives and the economic underclass
and at the same time weaken the voices calling for greater social, political and economic freedom. Heavy sanctions are
likely to strengthen the hands of the Iranian leaders who have
opposed the liberal economic reforms of the [previous lead-
ers] Rafsanjani and Khatami era and favor a return to the
controlled economy of the 1980s, when the government rather
than markets decided on the allocation of foreign exchange,

credit, and even basic necessities. The sanctions on gasoline imports under review may be a godsend for President Ahmadinejad, who would use the sanctions as an excuse to raise gasoline prices to the middle class and use the proceeds to expand his popular base.

Crippling sanctions could still change the balance of power against the Ahmadinejad government if the stresses caused by badly run government services and waiting in long lines for basic necessities were to bring the middle class into greater conflict with the government. But the principal victim of sanctions would not be the middle class, but the lower classes who may rally around the government in greater numbers. Economic pain caused from the outside is unlikely to weaken a populist government.

Setting the Stage for Engagement with Iran

If general sanctions are blunt tools for foreign policy, can smart sanctions help change the balance of power inside Iran by targeting specific industries and sections of the population? As with smart bombs, we should expect the case being made before their deployment to be rosier than the actual outcome.

Against this backdrop, engagement, as originally espoused by President Obama, may have a better chance of diffusing the crisis. First, if Iran is as close to nuclear capability as it is claimed, it should have a strong interest in non-proliferation. Making it difficult for a newcomer to join the nuclear club would enhance the value of its own potential membership and dissuade rivals from taking a similar path. If a major goal of sanctions against Iran is to dissuade other countries from taking the path to nuclear capability that Iran has taken, the possibility to make that case with "Iran as a partner" should be kept in mind if the strategy of "Iran as a victim" falls apart. Second, the U.S. and its allies should emphasize positive inducements, and expect to learn during the negotiations what those are rather than decide in advance. U.S. help for Iran to join the World Trade Organization (WTO), which has been offered before and which would benefit some sections of Iranian society while not others, is not a priority for the Ahmadinejad government. Third, it would help the engagement process if the U.S. acknowledged that Iran has something to offer the region in terms of lessons for economic development and building infrastructure—roads, electricity, education and health. This would have the added benefit of shifting the focus from Iran's military role in the region to economic development, which is the long term road to regional stability that both countries seek.

> *"However long and difficult the struggle may be, America should press for regime change, overtly and covertly, while taking care not to taint the people we seek to enable by making them look like tools of Uncle Sam."*

The United States Should Support an Iranian Regime Change

John R. Bolton

In the viewpoint that follows, John R. Bolton analyzes the four main options the United States has in contending with an Iranian regime bent on developing nuclear capabilities. Bolton claims that doing nothing or pursuing nonproductive diplomacy is tantamount to tolerating a nuclear Iran. Alternately, taking an aggressive military stance may hold Iranian nuclear programs in check but would assuredly not obliterate them, Bolton asserts. Instead, Bolton maintains that supporting regime change would be the "most durable solution" to the problem. He believes that young Iranians are ready to dispense with the Islamic government and negotiate with the modern world. Bolton insists that

John R. Bolton, "Iran Outlook: Grim," *National Review*, vol. 61, October 19, 2009, pp. 30–32. Copyright © 2009 by National Review, Inc., 215 Lexington Avenue, New York, NY 10016. Reproduced by permission.

America should do all it can to openly and secretly promote revolution as quickly as possible. A senior fellow at the American Enterprise Institute for Public Policy Research, Bolton is a conservative political analyst who served as the U.S. ambassador to the United Nations in 2005–2006.

As you read, consider the following questions:

1. According to Bolton, when did President Obama learn of the presence of a uranium-enrichment plant in Qom? Why does the timing of Obama's enlightenment bother Bolton?

2. What percentage of the Iranian population is under 30 years old, as Bolton relates?

3. What shift in power does Bolton see as evident in the crackdown following the June 12, 2009, presidential elections in Iran?

The week of September 21 [2009] was supposed to be multilateralism on parade for President [Barack] Obama: attending the Climate Summit, addressing the U.N. [United Nations] General Assembly, chairing the Security Council, and celebrating a new international economic order with the G-20 [a group of twenty finance ministers from around the world]. Until Friday, everything went according to Obama's script: grandiose speeches, paper declarations and resolutions, and, most important, the huzzahs of foreign leaders and America's media.

But on Friday, the shadow fell. Obama scrambled to hold a previously unscheduled press conference with British prime minister Gordon Brown and French president Nicolas Sarkozy, at which they announced that Iran had constructed a uranium-enrichment facility near Qom, the Shiite holy city. Housed in deeply buried chambers on a former missile base of the Iranian Revolutionary Guard Corps (IRGC), the site had been officially disclosed to the International Atomic Energy Agency (IAEA) by Iran that Monday, making it inevitable that word would leak out soon. (Iran risibly claims that the Qom facility is for civilian purposes only.)

The president was obviously displeased with Iran's contumacious behavior, and perhaps more displeased with the timing of his forced public disclosure of it, coming just before an October 1 meeting in Geneva between Iran and the Security Council's five permanent members [China, France, Russia, the United Kingdom, and the United States] plus Germany (the "Perm Five plus one"). This session, the first since summer 2008, and the first in which a U.S. representative would actively "engage" with Iran, had been intended to showcase Obama's multilateral bona fides [Latin term meaning "in good faith" or good intentions]. Now, however, Iran had threatened the carefully constructed mirage of negotiations with inconvenient reality.

A Change in President but No Change in Policy

According to administration background briefings, Obama was first informed about the Qom site during the transition following his election. Thus, all his pronouncements about the virtues of negotiation with Iran and other rogue states—the inaugural address, the Cairo speech, and countless others, including those of U.N. Week—were delivered with the knowledge that Iran was telling lies about its nuclear program. We shall soon see whether Obama's ability to hold two contradictory thoughts simultaneously is evidence of mental agility or of an excessively tenuous acquaintance with reality.

The administration's spin, dutifully amplified by the media, was that revealing the Qom enrichment facility was yet another Obama triumph, since it put more diplomatic pressure on Iran just before the Geneva meeting. Adhering to this logic requires believing that progressing toward a nuclear-weapons capability actually harms Iran, by increasing the risk of economic sanctions. If Iran tests a nuclear device, that will really put pressure on Iran, and incinerating Tel Aviv will presumably make the pressure for sanctions unstoppable. As [Greek historian] Plutarch quoted [Greek king and general] Pyrrhus as saying upon his defeat of the Romans at Asculum [which also brought major losses for the Greeks], "One more such victory and we are lost."

Sad to say, Obama's Iran policy is not much different from that of George W. Bush in his second term. Relying on multilateral negotiations (the Perm Five-plus-one mechanism), resorting to sanctions (three Security Council resolutions), and shying away from the use of force are all attributes inherited directly from Bush. Bush's policy failed to rein in Iran's nuclear ambitions, and Obama's will fail no less, leading to an Iran with nuclear weapons.

The issue now, however, is not this bipartisan history of failure, but what to do next. The Qom disclosure only highlights just how limited, risky, and unattractive are the four basic options: allow Iran to become a nuclear power; use diplomacy and sanctions to try to avert that outcome; remove the regime in Tehran [Iran's capital] and install one that renounces nuclear weapons; or use preemptive military force to break Iran's nuclear program. Let us consider them in turn.

Option 1: Doing Nothing

The easiest course, which Obama may well be on without explicitly admitting it, is to permit Iran to become a nuclear-weapons power. Many believe that a nuclear Iran will not constitute a significant threat, and that it can be contained and deterred, as the Soviet Union was during the Cold War. This analogy is fundamentally flawed. First, who in his right mind would willingly return to the days of mutual assured destruction, especially when the Tehran end of the equation is staffed by religious fanatics who prize the hereafter more than life on earth? It may not have been a virtue, but at least the Communists believed they went around only once. (A [country music singer] Kenny Chesney song sums up the predominant U.S. view: "Everybody want to go to Heaven / But nobody want to go now.") Moreover, we increasingly appreciate that Cold War deterrence was not all that stable, and therefore just how lucky we were to last 40 years without civilization-ending nuclear exchanges. That Iran in the near future will have a much more limited offensive-weapons capability than the Soviet Union did in its prime is no solace. Iran's asymmetric threat will not comfort those in cities that will have been obliterated by its "limited" arsenal. . . .

Option 2: Pursuing Diplomacy

Pursuing diplomacy and impotent sanctions was Bush's policy and is now Obama's. The only material difference is that Obama has even less reason than Bush had to believe that diplomacy may yet work. Iran's credibility after its rigged June 12 [2009] presidential election and the news about Qom is, yet again, in shreds everywhere—except the White House, where the public evidence of Obama's first eight months shows not the slightest diminution of his near-religious faith in diplomacy. Thus, the outcome of his efforts will be the same as Option 1, although few will say so.

Within the diplomatic approach, there is one hidden trap for the credulous: that Washington [D.C.] will accept the existence of an Iranian uranium-enrichment program as long as it is (supposedly) monitored by the IAEA under clear Iranian commitments that the program is (supposedly) entirely peaceful. One can easily envision Obama describing such an outcome as a triumph for his diplomacy, even though in fact it is exactly where we are today, and would inevitably lead to precisely the result we are trying to avoid. Any resolution that leaves Iran's current regime with control over the entire nuclear fuel cycle is simply a face-saving way of accepting Option 1. Given Iran's fulsome 20-year history of denial and deception, there is simply no doubt that its efforts toward building nuclear weapons would continue. If the Qom revelation does anything, it should convince us that Iran's commitments are worthless. . . .

Option 3: Promoting Regime Change

The most durable solution would be regime change in Iran that entirely sweeps away the Islamic Revolution of 1979—not just [President Mahmoud] Ahmadinejad, but the whole crew of [leader of the 1979 Revolution that overthrew the Iranian monarchy] Ayatollah Khomeini's successors. Iran's people are ready for this, as the regime is highly unpopular for many reasons. First, the mullahs [Islamic clergy] have mismanaged the economy for 30 years, and dissatisfaction is intense and widespread. Second, the two-thirds of Iran's population that is under 30 is well-educated and aware of the world outside Iran; they know they could have a radically different kind of life under a different government. Third, ethnic Persians make up only half the total population, and the numerous other groups (including Arabs, Baluchis, Azeris, Kurds, and Turkmen) are deeply discontented. Obviously, these fissures do not align exactly, but they are severe enough that the Islamic Revolution would not survive long without military force behind it.

The spontaneous protests that broke out across Iran following the fraudulent June 12 presidential election demonstrated both the extent of the opposition and the possibilities for regime change. Unfortunately, the post–June 12 results also reflect a tragic missed opportunity to topple the regime, and the difficulty of regaining that chance. Had the Bush administration taken more than a few trifling steps to aid the opposition, the post–June 12 protests might well have brought a new Iranian government. Apart from White House rhetoric, however, Bush's eight years differed little in hard operational terms from Obama's eight months, meaning that Iran's protesters were basically on their own. Moreover, political power

Iranians Support Regime Change

The United States should encourage regime change ... in Iran by espousing a policy ... of reconciliation and restoration by assisting the people of Iran in restoring [Prime Minister Mohammed] Mossadeq's secular democracy [1951–1953] which was interrupted by a U.S.-U.K. [United Kingdom] orchestrated and financed coup in 1953. The U.S. apologized in 2000. The U.S. should alert the people of Iran that an indigenous uprising against the mullahs [Islamic clergy] and the Revolutionary Guards would be supported by U.S. military strikes if requested by the freedom fighters themselves. Probably 90% of Iranians despise the mullahs. The vast majority covet the secular democracy of Mossadeq, a conclusion supported in part by the 1997 presidential vote repudiating the mullahs. Iran is not Iraq or Afghanistan. It has had more than a century of constitutionalism since 1906, and features a political culture conducive to democracy, including trade, student, and professional unions, a popular craving for a free press, and a highly literate and young population. There will be no Velvet Revolution [that is, non-violent] a la Eastern Europe because the mullahs are much more brutal and fanatical than Eastern Europe's communist leaders. They are more sophisticated than the United States predicted. Further, Eastern Europe was throwing off a Soviet yoke. Iran's mullahs and Revolutionary Guards would be defending their own country. . . . They will fight to the finish.

Mahtub Hojjati interviewed by Ryan Mauro,
"Regime Change in Iran: Interview with Mahtub Hojjati,"
Global Politician, *July 18, 2007. www.globalpolitician.com.*

inside Iran is shifting away from clerical leaders and toward the IRGC, moving from a theological autocracy toward military control. The balance of power rests with those holding guns. The regime's willingness to use force and political coercion against dissidents will be greater than it was before June 12, thus making it even harder to get rid of.

This is not to suggest the regime's popularity has increased. To the contrary, the regime is even more unpopular than it was before June 12, but the chances of a "velvet revolution" [i.e., non-violent revolution] in the foreseeable future are remote. But however long and difficult the struggle may be, America should press for regime change, overtly and covertly, while taking care not to taint the people we seek to enable by making them look like tools of Uncle Sam. Overthrowing the Islamic Revolution is the most likely way to obtain a government that permanently renounces nuclear weapons, which would be the best outcome. Almost certainly, however, regime change will not happen before Iran's current rulers acquire such weapons—and once that happens, it may be too late, both within Iran and for the Middle East and the rest of the world.

Option 4: Using Military Force

That leads, by process of elimination if nothing else, to the preemptive use of military force against Iran's nuclear infrastructure. No one argues that a successful strike would end the Iran problem, but that is not the point. Destroying key aspects of Iran's program (such as the Esfahan uranium-conversion plant, the Natanz uranium-enrichment facility, the Arak heavy-water complex, and the Bushehr reactor) would buy time. Between two and five years is a reasonable estimate, and that is close to eternity, because during that period time would be on our side rather than on the proliferator's.

President Obama is all but certain not to use force, so any decision regarding this option now rests with Israel alone. The revelation of the Qom site, and the risk that Iran has even more covert nuclear-related sites, may mean that the military option is already no longer viable: Destroying the known elements of Iran's program will be risky and difficult enough, but the prospect of more unknown sites means that targeted military force cannot be relied upon to completely break Iran's control over the nuclear fuel cycle. Israel would thus incur all the downsides of the attack without achieving its main goal. . . .

With so many risks of failure and retaliation, the use of military force is hardly attractive to Israel or anyone else. Even so, the consequences of a nuclear Iran could be far more devastating. Israel has not hesitated to strike preemptively before, starting with the Six-Day War of 1967, and including the destruction of the Osirak reactor outside Baghdad [Iraq] in 1981 and the North Korean reactor in Syria in September 2007. Don't bet on passivity now.

Iran's nuclear-weapons program has cast a shadow over its region and the world for years. That kind of regime, with those kinds of weapons, is a continuing mortal threat to America's friends and allies, and to international peace and security. Under President Bush, we had a chance to confront Iran's challenge, but backed away from it. Under President Obama, we have a leader who doesn't understand the magnitude of the threat, who flinches at unpleasant choices regarding force, and who believes that reductions of America's own nuclear arsenal will persuade the IRGC to give up theirs. If Iran achieves its nuclear objectives, we will have only ourselves to blame.

> "[Regime change] is a dangerous caprice that, if adopted as policy, would be ineffective at best and seriously damaging to American interests at worst."

The United States Should Not Support an Iranian Regime Change

Ted Galen Carpenter and Jessica Ashooh

In the following viewpoint, Ted Galen Carpenter and Jessica Ashooh argue that the United States would be foolish to fund or orchestrate regime change in Iran. According to the authors, Iranians are wary of U.S. involvement in their country, and even those who dislike the current clerical regime would be disinclined to aid America in overturning the government. Furthermore, Carpenter and Ashooh claim that the anti-regime agitators that the United States would likely have to support to topple the regime are a dubious lot whose goals are questionable and whose character is suspect. Carpenter and Ashooh contend that if the aim of U.S. policy is to thwart nuclear progress in Iran, then the proper way of achieving that end is to offer incentives that the Iranians cannot refuse, not to anger the entire nation by master-

Ted Galen Carpenter and Jessica Ashooh, "A View to a Coup?" The *National Interest*, March–April 2007, pp. 62–66. Copyright © 2007 The National Interest, Washington, D.C. Reproduced by permission.

minding a coup. Ted Galen Carpenter is vice president of Foreign Policy and Defense Studies at the Cato Institute, a libertarian public policy and research organization. Jessica Ashooh is an international studies scholar at Oxford University.

As you read, consider the following questions:

1. What is the MEK and why do Carpenter and Ashooh question its usefulness in aiding U.S. policy objectives in Iran?

2. According to the authors, what fact have neoconservatives overlooked when pointing fingers at the clerical regime for initiating Iran's nuclear program?

3. Although some analysts believe a nuclear-but-democratic Iran would ease U.S. fears, what do Carpenter and Ashooh insist is still problematic about this outcome?

Throughout Washington [D.C.'s] impasse with Iran, many influential Americans have viewed regime change as a panacea that would revoke the country's Axis of Evil membership and turn it into a bastion of democracy. Such thinking gained prominence in the past year [2006–2007], as the prospect of a diplomatic solution became a great deal murkier. Given the disappointing progress of the EU-3 [European Union-3: France, Germany, and the United Kingdom] negotiations, it seems unlikely that Iran will give up its nuclear program voluntarily. The question is how to deal with this refusal.

Most neoconservatives favor regime change, and they usually argue such an operation is possible without extensive U.S. military involvement. According to these proponents, there is so much domestic opposition to the religious elite that a U.S. propaganda offensive, combined with financial and logistical assistance to prospective insurgents, would topple the clerics. Michael Ledeen of the American Enterprise Institute has boasted, "I have contacts in Iran, fighting the regime. Give me twenty million [dollars] and you'll have your revolution."

The initial stage of the regime-change strategy got under way with the 2005 passage of the Iran Freedom Support Act, followed by a dramatic funding boost the next year. As Secretary of State Condoleezza Rice [of the George W. Bush administration] outlined, the expanded program primarily funds radio broadcasts and other propaganda activities, and it provides modest support for trade unions and other dissident groups.

Despite the enthusiasm, is regime change really a feasible or worthwhile strategy? And would it actually end [Iran's capital] Tehran's quest for nuclear weapons, much less nuclear technology? Evidence indicates that the answer to both questions is a firm no.

Allies of Questionable Character

The regime-change-from-within thesis might seem more plausible had we not heard it before in the run-up to the Iraq War. Indeed, the argument for regime change and the strategy embodied in the Iran Freedom Support Act are eerily reminiscent of Iraq policy between 1998 and 2003. Congress passed and funded an Iraq Liberation Act during that period. American policymakers believed the propaganda of Ahmad Chalabi and the Iraqi National Congress [INC] that—with modest financial and logistical support—Iraqi dissidents could overthrow the Saddam Hussein regime. It is now apparent that the INC never had more than a meager domestic following, and Chalabi's party garnered less than 0.5 percent of the votes in the December 2005 Iraqi parliamentary elections.

There are manipulative (and in some cases utterly objectionable) Iranian exiles waiting in the wings to orchestrate a similar scenario. They include notorious arms dealer Manucher Ghorbanifar, a shadowy figure from the Iran-Contra scandal. Perhaps the most unsavory opposition group is the Mujaheddin-e-Khalq (MEK), included on the U.S. State Department's list of terrorist organizations since 1997.

The MEK is the military wing of the National Council of Resistance of Iran (NCRI), regarded by many neoconservatives as a key ally in the regime change effort. Moving its base of operations from France to Iraq in 1986, the MEK was reportedly funded by Saddam Hussein's Ba'athi regime and sent into combat against Iran. Founded on a combination of Islamism and Marxism, the MEK has a long history of terrorism and cult-like behavior. Currently led by a married couple, Massoud and Maryam Rajavi, the organization has become a cult of personality, repeatedly purging individuals from its inner circle. As journalist Connie Bruck notes: "When, in June 2003, Maryam was arrested and imprisoned in France, several of her followers in Europe immolated themselves. Today, images of Maryam and Massoud Rajavi gaze out from walls in M.E.K. offices and barracks in Iraq and adorn placards and T-shirts at M.E.K. demonstrations." There is also a distressing amount of regimentation. The organization mandates vows of celibacy in its Iraqi camps, and it ruthlessly suppresses dissent from the Rajavis' dictates. Former MEK members report that comrades who sought to leave were imprisoned or killed.

That reputation does not discourage some regime change proponents from making common cause with MEK activists. In May 2003, scholars Daniel Pipes and Patrick Clawson of the Washington Institute for Near East Policy recommended that "when the secretary of state next decides whether or not to re-certify the MEK as a terrorist organization", that official "should come to the sensible conclusion that it poses no threat to the security of the United States or its citizens." Pipes and Clawson went on to praise the MEK as a potential ally, citing the organization's "key information" about Iran's nuclear program and other activities.

Lingering Ill Will Against American Involvement

Setting aside the wisdom of supporting groups like the MEK, Americans should doubt assurances that significant U.S. military assistance would be unnecessary. In the case of Iraq, regime change advocates quietly buried such assurances when they became impatient with Saddam Hussein's continuing power. Saddam's overthrow required massive U.S. military power, with the much-touted exiles playing the role of embarrassing hangers-on. If the United States adopts a strategy of regime change in Iran, it too will demand extensive U.S. efforts.

There is little doubt that Iranians increasingly dislike the repressive mullahs [religious leaders]—but that does not make them fond of the United States, a 2006 Zogby poll found. A good many Iranians remember that the United States interfered once before in their country's internal affairs (the 1953 coup), and that the outcome was not a happy one. Moreover, virtually all populations resent pressure and interference from foreign powers. Citizens typically rally around the incumbent regime and reject opposition figures tainted by foreign influence, even if the public might normally be sympathetic to those reformers' political values—and in this case, most Iranians regard the MEK as a collection of odious terrorists, and evidence of Washington's collaboration with such elements would be especially resented.

Some Iranian dissidents are very nervous that open American endorsements could be the kiss of death. Washington's support gives the religious hierarchy a perfect pretext to portray even cautious political reformers as American stooges. Iranian human rights activist Emad Baghi complained: "We are under pressure from both the hard-liners in the judiciary and that stupid George Bush." Vahid Pourostad, editor of the pro-reform *National Trust* newspaper, noted that whenever the United States "supported an idea publicly, the public has done the opposite."

Force Will Not Dislodge the Iranian Regime

Perhaps the regime change thesis's most bizarre incarnation is the notion that military intervention is a needed catalyst. By this line of thinking, the Iranian people would be so enraged at the clerics for bringing destruction upon them that they would overthrow the regime. *Weekly Standard* editor Bill Kristol is most explicit with this rationale. Asserting that "the Iranian people dislike their regime", he predicted on Fox News in July 2006 that "the right use of military force could cause them to reconsider whether they really want to have this regime in power."

The historical record lends this logic—dubious on its face—little support. Bombing Iran would almost certainly be counterproductive to the goal of regime change. One only need look back a few months, to the surge in [Shiite terrorist organization] Hizballah's popularity during the Israeli incursion into Lebanon, to realize that such thinking is naive. Earlier episodes point to a similar conclusion. Despite massive bombing of Germany and Japan in World War II, the fascist regimes remained in power to the bitter end. The American bombing of North Vietnam in the 1960s and early 1970s did not dislodge Ho Chi Minh or his successors from power. NATO's [North Atlantic Treaty Organization] bombing of Serbia in 1999 actually *increased* Slobodan Milosevic's popularity for a time. It was not until one year later, and based on domestic issues, that the democratic opposition got rid of him.

A Change in Government Does Not Ensure a Change in Nuclear Agenda

Still, it is possible that the most ardent supporters of a regime-change policy would be willing to roll the dice. But there is one problem with the regime change strategy that cannot be ignored: Even if the United States brought a secular, democratic government to power, said government would not necessarily end the nuclear program.

Positive Alternatives to Iran's Nuclear Program

The odds that sanctions will have an impact improve if the people of Iran are in the know. The goal is not to deny Iran a right to enrich uranium under international supervision. Nor is it to increase the hardship of the Iranian people. Rather, the world should make the argument that Iran could enjoy a higher standard of living, greater security and enhanced standing if it were to accept limits on its nuclear programme. It is important to portray Iran's nuclear activities as both unnecessary and a costly liability.

Richard N. Haass,
"A Different Regime Change in Iran,"
Financial Times, *October 13, 2009.*

Neoconservative policymakers have come to regard Iran's nuclear program as symptomatic of the clerical regime, while overlooking the fact that the American-backed shah [Mohammad Reza Pahlavi] founded the program under much more ostensibly martial auspices. Indeed, in 1967, the United States provided Tehran with a 5MW thermal research reactor—three years *before* Iran ratified the Nuclear Non-Proliferation Treaty (NPT). In one instance, the shah even affirmed the non-civilian nature of his country's nuclear ambitions, stating that Iran would develop nuclear weapons "without a doubt and sooner than one would think." Ironically, the Ayatollah Khomeini halted the program for several years after the Islamic Revolution, deeming nuclear weapons contrary to Islam.

Iran is located in a volatile and hostile region. Iranians are still emotionally scarred by Iraq's 1980 invasion and the long, bloody war that followed. Russia, Israel, Pakistan and India all have nuclear weapons, so regional deterrence issues probably loom large for Tehran. Those security concerns would not change significantly for a democratic government.

Moreover, the vast majority of Iranian citizens seem to favor an indigenous nuclear program, whether for solely peaceful purposes or not—whatever the consequences. According to a January 2006 poll by the Iranian Students Polling Agency, 85 percent of Iranians support the program. When told it would bring economic sanctions, 64 percent still supported the program. (After decades of American embargoes, sanctions no longer rattle the Iranian public. "The sanctions will be useless", insists one Tehran resident. "We do not have much foreign investment now either.") However, the poll's most striking finding is that 56 percent of respondents supported the program in the face of a military strike. And should that strike take place, "only one in six would blame Iran's own government" for precipitating it.

To be sure, hefty doses of state propaganda influence such opinions. Yet even reformers support the program. Nobel peace laureate Shirin Ebadi, a liberal Iranian critic, warned Washington not to attack: "We will defend our country till the last drop of blood." Those are the words of a pro-Western, liberal Iranian, so one can only imagine what those less hostile to the current government think.

Iranians Are Proud of Their Nuclear Program

The nuclear program has come to symbolize Iranian scientific prestige, upon which the nation prides itself in a way somewhat surprising for such a conservative state. For example, Iranian scientists performing stem cell research receive government funding and enjoy one of the most broadly permissive policies in the world, orders of magnitude more so than current American regulations that effectively prohibit federal funding. In terms of the national psyche, this scientific prowess represents Iran's global and regional influence, which most Iranians believe should be robust.

It is apparent that the Iranian nuclear program has come to embody more than the odious regime that stewards it. The broad support renders the question of what to do particularly difficult, as it is almost certain the program will continue with or without Western approval, no matter what regime is in power. Indeed a new, democratic government might find itself under considerable popular pressure to demonstrate nationalist credentials—and prove it is not a U.S. puppet.

True, if a nuclear-armed Iran were democratic, it would significantly ease Washington's concerns that the country might pose an undeterrable threat to America's security. Michael Ledeen told the House International Relations Committee that the nuclear threat "is inseparable from the nature of the regime." If the clerical regime were not in power, there would not be such a "sense of urgency." On another occasion, Ledeen conceded that a democratic Iran might continue a quest for nuclear weapons, but that "a democratic Iran will not be inclined to commit hara-kiri by launching a first strike against Israel, nor will it likely brandish its bombs against the United States." Robert Kagan, a senior associate at the Carnegie Endowment for International Peace, states: "Were Iran ruled by even an imperfect democratic government, we would be much less concerned about its weaponry."

But even a democratic Iran with nukes would undermine another major U.S. policy goal: preventing further nuclear proliferation. There is a very real prospect that if Iran develops a nuclear arsenal, sooner or later other countries in the region, such as Saudi Arabia, Egypt and Turkey, would follow suit. And it is unlikely to make much difference to these countries whether a nuclear-capable Iran is democratic or undemocratic. What will matter is that a regional rival has that capability.

Regime Change Would Be Difficult and Costly

The regime change option is a fantasy maintained by those enamored with their own ideology. It has no realistic chance of toppling the Iranian regime or halting nuclear proliferation. On the contrary, it is a dangerous caprice that, if adopted as policy, would be ineffective at best and seriously damaging to American interests at worst. The only way to prevent the nuclearization of any country is through incentives that make non-proliferation more attractive than nuclear weaponry. In the case of Iran, this means addressing the country's security concerns and vibrant nationalism, rather than inflaming them. Such realism, though, means abandoning the illusion that regime change would be an easy and definitive solution.

Periodical Bibliography

The following articles have been selected to supplement the diverse views presented in this chapter.

Riccardo Alcaro	"Tempting Tehran," *World Today*, July 2009.
Jonathan Broder	"Neutral on Iran Today for Diplomacy Tomorrow," *CQ Weekly*, June 22, 2009.
Allan C. Brownfield	"More and More Jewish Voices Opposing Israel-Promoted Pre-Emptive Attack on Iran," *Washington Report on Middle East Affairs*, August 2009.
Steve Coll	"No Nukes," *New Yorker*, April 20, 2009.
Michael Crowley	"Iran Amok," *New Republic*, March 18, 2009.
Newt Gingrich	"Forget Negotiations, President Obama, Seize the Moment," *Human Events*, June 29, 2009.
Max Rodenbeck	"The Iran Mystery Case," *New York Review of Books*, January 15, 2009.
Laura Secor	"Keep Away," *New Republic*, April 23, 2007.
Gerald F. Seib	"Rules on Iran Haven't Changed," *Wall Street Journal*, June 16, 2009.
Michael Spies	"Solving the Iran Nuclear Situation Peaceably: An Update on the Dual Track Approach," *Peace Magazine*, October–December 2009.

OPPOSING VIEWPOINTS® SERIES

CHAPTER 3

What Was the Impact of the 2009 Iranian Presidential Election?

Chapter Preface

The June 2009 presidential election in Iran pitted four candidates against each other for the executive position in the Tehran government. Mahmoud Ahmadinejad was the incumbent candidate representing a union of conservative parties. He had won his first term as president in 2005 and quickly gained an international reputation as a hardliner who favored Iran's nuclear program; supported religious traditionalism; and openly criticized Israel, the United States, and other Western nations for meddling in Middle Eastern affairs. Ahmadinejad was joined on the conservative platform by Mohsen Rezaei, the former chief commander of the Islamic Revolutionary Guard Corps, an ideologically motivated military elite that serves the revolutionary government. In his campaign, Rezaei asserted that he would try to restore Iran's economy, which he said was brought to the "edge of a precipice" by the incumbent candidate. Rezaei also called for better relations with the United States in order to keep peace in the region.

The two "reformist" candidates who ran in the 2009 election were Mehdi Karroubi and Mir Hossein Mousavi. The chairman of the National Trust Party and former parliament leader, Karroubi is a moderate reformer who promised greater attention to human rights—including the expansion of women's rights—and advocated for the nationalization of oil revenues. Like Rezaei, Karroubi also earned support by challenging Ahmadinejad's economic policies. In pre-election television debates (reiterated on the American Free Press on June 6, 2009), Karroubi insisted that the president was disseminating inaccurate growth and unemployment statistics, claiming, "All the figures that you have given are contradictory to the ones we [in the parliament] have seen over the years."

Mir Hossein Mousavi formerly served as the prime minister of Iran (from 1981 to 1989) and is currently the president of the Iranian Academy of Arts. Another critic of Ahmadinejad's economic strategy, Mousavi, too, publically accused the reigning president of hiding the dire state of Iran's fiscal outlook. He gained widespread support in Iran for opposing government corruption, championing greater personal freedoms, and calling for a review of some of the legal barriers that hamper women's rights. Mousavi, however, did not run as a reformist candidate; instead he called himself an independent, gladly welcoming support from the reformist camp. And while many observers inside and outside Iran saw him as a preferable alternative to the uncompromising Ahmadinejad, a few questioned whether Mousavi's policies would be vastly different from those of the sitting president. Mousavi, in fact, still backed the clerical regime, and he pushed for the peaceful expansion of Iran's nuclear program. "We will not accept our country's deprivation from the right to nuclear energy," Mousavi informed *Time* magazine on June 11, 2009.

On June 12, election day, the Iranian government declared Ahmadinejad the winner after only two-thirds of the poll results had been tallied. The incumbent garnered 62 percent of the vote, while Mousavi, the closest contender, received 34 percent. Immediately after the announcement, supporters of Mousavi and Karroubi leveled charges of fraud, insisting that the votes could not have been counted so quickly and that the results showed irregularities in areas where pre-election canvassing showed mass support for the reformist candidates. Thousands of Iraqis took to the streets to protest the vote count, in response, the government called out riot police to end rioting in Tehran, Iran's capital, on the weekend after the election. The clerical leader, Ayatollah Ali Khamenei, ordered an investigation into the proceedings and a partial recount. Finding no irregularities, the recount officials endorsed Ahmadinejad's victory.

With the Iranian government experiencing internal division and mass opposition, some Western observers believe the time for regime change in Iran is close at hand. In the following chapter, several critics and commentators chart the impact of the controversial presidential election and the role it may play in cracking the closed society that still prevails in Iran.

> *"What started out as an outpouring of anger has turned into a battle royale for the soul of a nation."*

The 2009 Iranian Election Solidified the Opposition Movement

Hooman Majd

In June 2009, incumbent Iranian President Mahmoud Ahmadinejad won re-election amid claims of voting fraud and protests by supporters of opposition leader Mir Hossein Mousavi. In the following viewpoint, Hooman Majd asserts that the questionable outcome of the election has angered large sections of the Iranian populace. Majd insists that suspected interference in the democratic process, coupled with growing resistance to conservative rule, has united the opposition movement in Iran, perhaps sealing the fate of the present regime. Majd is a New York writer and author of The Ayatollah Begs to Differ.

As you read, consider the following questions:

1. What was the strategy of the Mousavi campaign from the beginning of the presidential race, according to Majd?

Hooman Majd, "Dawn of the Revolt," The *New Republic*, vol. 240, July 15, 2009, pp. 14–15. Copyright © 2009 by The New Republic, Inc. Reproduced by permission of The *New Republic*.

2. How does Majd describe President Ahmadinejad's victory rally?

3. In Majd's view, what most upset Iranians about the 2009 election?

*M*ay 23rd [2009]: [Iranian capital] Tehran's Azadi Indoor Stadium, 20 days before the election. The press had difficulty getting in the gates. "All full," the guards kept telling us. And full it was, overflowing in fact, for a Mir Hossein Mousavi [reformist candidate] campaign rally. Mousavi wasn't even there. Instead, the rally featured former President Mohammad Khatami and Mousavi's wife, Zahra Rahnavard, and the eager crowd numbered more than 20,000. I couldn't make my way to the VIP section, and I didn't want to. I was happy to be crushed among the thousands of cheering—ecstatic even— Iranians who gave birth to the "green wave."

It was not supposed to end like this. After all, this is why Khatami, the only early favorite to defeat [the current president Mahmoud] Ahmadinejad at the polls on June 12, dropped out of the presidential race, isn't it? That's what we all assumed in the weeks and days leading up to 6/12 [election day]. Yes, 6/12. Khatami would never be allowed to win. *Kayhan*, Iran's conservative daily and the Supreme Leader's mouthpiece, said as much, even threatening him, in a thinly veiled editorial, with assassination.

A Gathering Opposition Movement

Mir Hossein Mousavi, we thought, posed no such threat to the conservatives—the landlords, let's call them. His chances of winning weren't exactly good, even as recently as six weeks before the election. "If the turnout is in the twenty-five-million range, we will be guests of Mr. Ahmadinejad for another four years." That was Sadegh Kharrazi—former ambassador to Paris, deputy foreign minister, and an influential reformist who also has close ties to the Supreme Leader—speaking at the end of April. It was another late-night salon at his house, filled with photos of himself with Ayatollah Khamenei [the supreme religious leader of Iran]. "Ahmadinejad has ten to twelve million votes," he said, a number echoed by virtually everyone I spoke to, "and he'll win if the turnout is low." He wasn't being pessimistic—just realistic. I was a realist then, too.

The Mousavi campaign's early strategy, one of getting out the vote to counter Ahmadinejad's solid base, raised no eyebrows, but it began to pay dividends, and a fever for the democratic process started to afflict many previously apathetic Iranians. "If the majority doesn't vote, the minority rules," proclaimed billboards, rather more poetically in Persian, that I saw all over town at the end of May. Ayatollah Rafsanjani [another former president of Iran, 1987–1997] had paid for that one, his image next to the words. If the fever held, there would be enough votes to force a second-round runoff. Mousavi was going to win any runoff, and win big. Ahmadinejad might have his ten to twelve million, but he couldn't possibly defeat Mousavi if the entire opposition coalesced around one candidate. It wasn't as if Ahmadinejad's campaign didn't know this. Its strategy from the start had been to win outright in the first round, but his campaign was anemic compared to Mousavi's, which grew stronger by the rally, with the ever-popular Khatami front and center much of the time. I almost went with Khatami to Ahvaz, on May 30, when the plane he was to have caught back to Tehran was discovered to have a bomb aboard. The landlords weren't whispering anymore. They had never seriously fought this kind of battle before. "If it's over thirty million, [we win]," Khatami had said to me in mid-May over tea in his office in a villa in Jamaran, Ayatollah Khomeini's old compound in North Tehran. "Are you staying for the election?" he asked me. "No, but I'll come back for the second round," I told him. "There won't be a second round; we will win outright on June 12." Strong words coming from a cautious man two weeks before the election.

Ahmadinejad's Anemic Support

And, based on what I had seen in Iran over the last month, maybe Khatami was right. I tried, really tried, to find where Ahmadinejad's support was going to come from if he was going to add to his base, to defeat three challengers who were all gaining popularity. Outside of Tehran? Whether on the road, or in truck stops, cafes, and other cities, I saw more enthusiasm for the opposition than for the president, which surprised me. Even in south Tehran, his supposed base in the capital, I found Ahmadinejad detractors. Not that Ahmadinejad didn't have supporters everywhere. It was just that they seemed to be apathetic. Perhaps that's the lot of an incumbent candidate steering a discontented nation. Not one Ahmadinejad supporter tried to convert me to their cause, or even bothered to make a compelling case. Maybe that's why the twelve million or so mythical Iranians who braved long lines, thunderstorms, and 100-degree-plus temperatures to vote for Mahmoud Ahmadinejad didn't celebrate on the streets when their man won his landslide. Even the ten or twelve million who probably *did* vote for him were reluctant to come out and cheer, at least until they were asked, two days later. And, even then, the photo of his victory rally was clumsily photoshopped, presumably by Mahmoud's experts, to illustrate a sea of Iranians for Ahmadinejad where there was only a pond.

Nearly 40 million voted in Iran's presidential election, 63 percent for the sitting president, according to his very own Interior Ministry. It took a day or so, but that's when it struck me and all the other dismayed Iranians: Of course, they were never going let *anyone* but Ahmadinejad win. That's why his campaign was anemic, that's why he didn't seem to care that his challengers were gaining on him. This had never happened before. Iranian elections have always been generally fair.

The Failure of Democracy Angers the Populace

Thirty years have passed since the revolution [1979 Islamic revolution in which monarchial leader Shah Mohammad Reza Pahlavi was overthrown and replaced by Ayatollah Ruhollah Khomeini and the Islamic Republic], exactly 30 years, and Iranians aren't mad that Ahmadinejad won reelection. They're mad that the one thing—the one and only element of democracy—they had left, their vote, is now meaningless. Stop looking at Tehran, the government keeps saying, you're misreading the country. You in the West don't understand Iran, it bleats; you don't know that Ahmadinejad really *did* have all the support of the country. It's only the Westernized elite in Tehran who are unhappy, and the West and Zionists (always the Zionists) are stirring things up. Iran's very own Useful Idiots in the West parrot their line, lending credence to outdated polls, to mathematical analyses that tell Iranians who are giving their lives for the right to a legitimate vote that they are dying for a lie. OK, then how about Shiraz, how about Isfahan, Mashhad, Tabriz, all the places we know people don't believe you, where people have *died* because they don't believe you? These Iranians didn't start by protesting the regime, the *nezam*, as the Supreme Leader called it; they weren't protesting anything but for their right to their vote. Mir Hossein Mousavi wasn't waging a campaign to bring down the nezam. He only wanted to be a better president than Ahmadinejad, to secure renters' rights in a nation of landlords, and that wasn't a crime until now.

What started out as an outpouring of anger has turned into a battle royale for the soul of a nation. Or a battle to allow the nation a soul. What delicious irony that Ayatollah Hashemi Rafsanjani, a founder of the *nezam*, a man Iranians couldn't bring themselves to vote for the last time, would be on the protestors' side. Who would have thought that Ali Larijani, speaker of Parliament, obedient son of the Revolution, and close confidant of the Supreme Leader, would suggest, in contradiction of his mentor, that the Guardian Council, which is supposed to be checking [on elections], has erred? Iran's leadership cracked, and the fissures are widening. The landlords' security teams might quell the protests, life may return to something resembling normal. The landlords still have a large portion of the population behind them, the ten to twelve million, maybe more, plus all the guns. (If the West, or Iranians in opposition movements abroad, try to hijack the protests for their own causes, they'll have more, much more.) And Mousavi, the unlikely hero of 6/12, may or may not continue the fight. But Iranians won't forget. They won't forget the dead, the prisoners, and the brutality of their landlords. At a pre-election press conference that I heard about, one Mousavi campaign manager was asked about the brutality of his *nezam*, way back, when he was prime minister in the 1980s. The staffer answered, "We were all Ahmadinejads then." After 6/12, we Iranians are all Mousavis now, even those who voted for Ahmadinejad, whether they know it yet or not.

> "[The] gap—between the green move-
> ment's leaders and the people in the
> streets—is widening."

The Opposition Movement
in Iran Is Not Unified

Mehdi Khalaji

*Mehdi Khalaji argues in the following viewpoint that the politi-
cal leaders of the reformist "green movement" in Iran are not in
tune with the revolutionary idealism of the constituents they
represent. As Khalaji explains, the 2009 reformist candidate, Mir
Hossein Mousavi, had no desire to see the theocratic rule of Iran
come to an end. Instead, had he won the presidential election, he
wished only to make simple policy changes while preserving the
system, Khalaji claims. However, in Khalaji's opinion, the true
green movement has far loftier goals of ending clerical rule and
restructuring the whole government. For this reason, Khalaji
contends that even if politicians like Mousavi ended up in power,
the more radical elements of the green movement would quickly
push them aside to enact the kind of sweeping change most Iranians desire. Khalaji is a senior fellow at the Washington Institute for Near East Policy.*

Mehdi Khalaji, "Who's Really Running Iran's Green Movement," *Foreign Policy*, November 4, 2009. Reproduced by permission.

As you read, consider the following questions:

1. According to Khalaji, how did the moderate reformist leaders end up as candidates for the green movement?

2. What two "notions" motivate the green movement, as the author states?

3. Who does Khalaji say are the true leaders of the green movement in Iran?

Nearly six months after the demonstrations that followed June's [2009] disputed presidential election, Iran's pro-democracy "green movement" is as strong as ever. Rallies took place in downtown [Iranian capital] Tehran today [November 4, 2009], having been in the works for months through Twitter, blogs, and word of mouth. Iran, it seems, is on the verge of having a new, unified opposition party.

But the solidarity on the streets hides wide—and growing—splits within. The ostensible leaders of the movement, Mir Hossein Mousavi, Mohammad Khatami, and Mehdi Karroubi, are former high-ranking officials of the Islamic Republic who would likely keep much about the Islamic Revolution in place. Contrast this with the young men and women on the streets, and you see differences that go beyond the generational. The protesters are aiming to bring down the very system of which their leaders are a part.

Green Party Candidates Are Only Moderate Reformists

Despite being lauded as modernizers, opposition front-runner Mousavi and his two green movement colleagues are deeply loyal to the ideals of Ayatollah Rouhollah Khomeini, the founder of the Islamic Republic, and advocate a theocratic political system. Had Mousavi come into office following the June 12 presidential election, he would not have challenged the political order. He would have tried to fix the Islamic

Republic's internal and external crises through slight policy tweaks. Nor would the West have seen an "opening" of the sort that some suggest. Indeed, Mousavi's rivalry with President Mahmoud Ahmadinejad has little to do with the current regime's foreign policy and far more to do with internal power struggles, economic policy, and, to some extent, cultural agendas. A new leader would not have fundamentally changed Iran's position on nuclear policy or its regional role. The reason is simple: Everyone who ran for president concedes that foreign-policy decisions should fall to Iran's supreme leader, Ayatollah Ali Khamenei.

So how did such moderates end up at the helm of a revolution? By accident. None of the reform candidates could have predicted that, following the mass vote-rigging during the presidential election, a popular movement would arise. These "leaders" had only a small role both in organizing and creating the movement, but they were swept into power by a spontaneous and improvised groundswell. The government had carefully vetted candidates, keeping anyone too reformist from running. So the grass-roots movement was left with a choice between two evils: Mousavi, the lesser one, and [incumbent President Mahmoud] Ahmadinejad.

Mousavi reluctantly became the symbolic leader of the green movement, but he, Karroubi, and Khatami remain aloof. Today's demonstrations, for example, were imagined and promoted by bloggers and leaders of human rights and women's movements for at least two months. It was only last week, after these plans were well circulated (and the Grand Ayatollah had warned against them), that Mousavi issued a statement calling for demonstrations on Nov. 4.

A Movement More Radical than Its Leaders

So today, these three former officials find themselves at the helm of a movement whose views they do not necessarily rep-

Supporting Change Without Supporting Violent Revolution

Dr. Mojtaba Mahdavi, an assistant professor of political science at the University of Alberta and an Iran expert, says the reform movement in Iran needs to be discussed at two levels, one at the state level, which is very much about power struggle within the establishment, and the other at the societal level, people who have a long history of quest for democracy and freedom.

"The fact is the reformist movement is far ahead of the reformist politicians in terms of their demands," he says, but the young generation, he adds, "don't like violence, they don't want to make a revolution, and they do cost benefit analysis."

If they think [Green movement leader Mir Hossein] Mousavi is going to bring some change for the better and get rid of Ahmadinejad and his policies, then they'd decide to take part in the elections, but this doesn't mean that they ideologically believe in all the points supported by Mousavi, he says.

Kamran Moradi,
"Iran's Green Movement: A Look into the Formation
of Reform Movement in Iran and the Power Struggle
within the Islamic Republic," Epoch Times,
August 17, 2009. www.theepochtimes.com.

resent. That gap—between the green movement's leaders and the people in the streets—is widening. Even in the midst of protests, there is growing discord. For instance, Mousavi and Karroubi have both criticized slogans like "No Gaza, no Lebanon—I sacrifice my life for Iran" as "extremist," despite their being a widespread feature of current popular action in Iran.

But the most fundamental split comes over what the movement makes of the Iranian Revolution. Mousavi and Khatami have reiterated their desired goal of returning to the ideals of late Ayatollah Khomenei and the original principles of the Islamic Republic. But those in the streets are conscious of the failure of past reforms and have little hope that the Islamic Republic—a system in which the supreme leader has the authority to veto both Islamic and national law—can be saved. And the green movement remains motivated by the notion of human rights and citizenship, both absent in Iran's Constitution. Hence, the part of the movement that first began to peacefully protest against the vote manipulation in this summer's election finds itself diametrically opposed to Ayatollah Khamenei and the Revolutionary Guard under him.

Khatami, a former president himself, is certainly cognizant of the split; in a recent speech, he tried to distinguish between those participating in current protests, who reject the entire existing system, and his own followers, who prefer to work within the political structure of the Islamic Republic with a ruling jurist above all.

But the bulk of the movement agrees less with the so-called leaders and more with the Islamic Republic's young third generation, who form 70 percent of the Iranian population and make up most of the demonstrators. The true leaders of this movement are students, women, human rights activists, and political activists who have little desire to work in a theocratic regime or in a government within the framework of the existing Constitution. This movement is much broader than the reform movement of the 1990s, when Khatami was president. Then, the number of people demanding reform on the streets never exceeded 50,000. According to Tehran's conservative mayor, Mohammad Baqer Qalibaf, more than 3 million people protested in the wake of this year's June 12 election.

If you want to know the unconventional nature of this movement—and what the people who have bravely taken to the streets really want—I don't listen to Mousavi, Karroubi, and Khatami.

Since the true representatives of reform owe little to them, a successful green movement would likely push them aside anyway.

This is why it is not only the regime in Tehran—but also the reformist "leaders" who pretend to lead this movement— that fear the success of the green movement. Democracy in Iran will emerge only through a rupture with the late Ayatollah Khomeini's ideals and Islamic ideology—concepts to which the accidental leaders of the green movement are still loyal.

> *"What seems evident as the crisis deepens is that a whole series of ideological beliefs and political institutions inherited from the revolution of 1979 are now put into question."*

The Iranian Government Is Facing a Crisis of Legitimacy

Ramin Jahanbegloo

Ramin Jahanbegloo argues in the following viewpoint that the fallout after accusations of voting fraud during the 2009 presidential election in Iran is having a devastating effect on the conservative government. As Jahanbegloo claims, the ruling Ayatollah's support for the incumbent president, Mahmoud Ahmadinejad, reveals a partisanship the populace is not likely to forget. In the author's view, the ruling cleric sacrificed some of his legitimacy as a spiritual leader by taking a hand in electoral affairs. Likewise, President Ahmadinejad's dismissal of the violent protests that followed his election and his crackdown on dissident voices will prompt many Iranians to question the legitimacy of a government that is supposed to be run on republican principles that cherish social justice and the right to political dis-

Ramin Jahanbegloo, "Legitimacy Crisis and the Future of Democracy in Iran," *Constellations: An International Journal of Critical & Democratic Theory*, vol. 16, September 2009, pp. 361–362. Copyright © 2009 Basil Blackwell Ltd. Reproduced by permission of Blackwell Publishers.

sent. *Jahanbegloo is a professor of political science at the University of Toronto in Canada. He previously headed the Department for Contemporary Studies in the Iranian Cultural Research Bureau.*

As you read, consider the following questions:

1. What is the historical role of the supreme leader, according to Jahanbegloo?

2. How does the author describe the motivations of the two types of young demonstrators who have taken to the streets after the June 2009 elections?

3. Why does Jahanbegloo believe that Iran cannot follow the same type of path to unification that China did after the Tiananmen Square showdown?

The massive public demonstrations of the past week in Iran [after the June 12, 2009, presidential elections], unprecedented since the revolution thirty years ago, have been seen as a battle between the supporters of Mir-Hossein Mousavi, the reformist challenger and the incumbent president, Mahmoud Ahmadinejad. Yet the current upheaval is about a much deeper struggle taking place in the corridors of power in [the Iranian capital] Tehran and it is likely to bring about a major transformation of the Islamic Republic. Certainly, a lot depends on the future moves of the political-religious-military-security leadership who control the levers of state violence, but what seems evident as the crisis deepens is that a whole series of ideological beliefs and political institutions inherited from the revolution of 1979 are now put into question. Among these, we find the cherished belief that the Islamic revolution removed tyranny and established a system of social justice. Actually, the regime's conduct in the past one week has presented serious challenges to its own political institutions while undermining its republican principles by granting no legitimacy to the judgment of the Iranian public sphere.

More generally, regardless of whether there was significant fraud in the presidential elections, those among the architects of the political establishment who believed that the system allowed scope of reform and change find themselves facing an authoritarian structure that uses extreme violence to ensure its political survival. Though the pre-reform clerics such as moderate former president Mohammad Khatami have increasingly warned Iran's conservative leadership of "dangerous consequences" if people were prevented from expressing their demands in nonviolent ways, the Supreme Leader, Ayatollah Khamenei, argued that to make concessions to popular demands and "illegal" pressure would amount to a form of "dictatorship" and warned the protestors that they, rather than the police, would be held responsible for any further violence.

The Establishment Shows Signs of Cracking

By clearly coming out in support of the conservative camp and acknowledging the fact that his views on foreign and domestic policy were closer to those of Ahmadinejad than to those of the president's foes and critics—although historically his role is to remain an arbiter and above factionalism— Ayatollah Khamenei publically jeopardized his political and spiritual legitimacy and the regime's armor invincibility, which are so central to the regime's authoritarian control. One needs also to add that none of the quietist clerics in Qom came forward to endorse either the election results or Ayatollah Khamenei's famous speech. In other words, the fissure appears to be expressing itself not only between the Iranian state and the young civil society, but also between the Supreme Leader and the Grand Ayatollahs in Qom. [Former president of Iran and current Ayatollah] Rafsanjani's opposition to Ahmadinejad has also raised speculation of possible rifts emerging in the ruling theocracy over the election. Rafsanjani heads the Assembly of Experts, a panel of clerics with the power to review the supreme leader's performance and remove him—

Regime Change Is Coming

In my view, a high [voter] turn-out ... meant the time for a coup d'etat [a successful uprising] was drawing closer....

The regime did not expect as big a participation as occurred and reacted with fraud, which was met with demonstrations.

The regime tried to frighten people through arrests and repression. The regime appears to have succeeded in doing that. But in the longer run, it will be different.

Something has happened. The regime's power is decreasing. The legitimacy of the regime has disappeared. This is important.

The movement continues. We will see little by little, things happening.

Parveen Ardalan interviewed by Raroog Sulehria,
"Iran: 'The Regime's Legitimacy Has Disappeared,'"
Green Left Weekly, *November 11, 2009.*

although that has never been used. Therefore, that the elections might or might not have been rigged is now a completely irrelevant question.

During the past few days [in September 2009] the unarmed and peaceful Iranians across all ages and classes have flocked to the streets of Tehran, defying brutal paramilitary squads, to demand major transformations in the structure of the political establishment in Iran. With such a complex landscape and fast-moving developments on the ground, Iran's political future has become even more obscure and uncertain than its immediate past. That said, an equally important fact is that most of the young demonstrators who have been questioning the legitimacy of Iran's electoral process, and now the credibility of the Iranian political institutions, are not, unlike their parents, interested in revolutionary upheaval or violent change. Some could be prepared to take their protests to the limit. Many others, however, have no interest in an all-out mutiny against the country's Islamic system. The protest movement, however, has appeared to gain some solid footing after days of street clashes that left different cities of Iran scorched and battered. The greatest degree of uncertainty surrounds a scenario in which the military elite conclude that the mass protests reflect deep-seated discontent and that a Tiananmen moment [referring to student uprising in China in 1989] is necessary.

Continuing Unrest in Iran's Future

Needless to say that Iran is incapable of following China's path. Twenty years after Tiananmen, the Chinese Communist Party has increased its popularity through delivering staggering economic growth and cultivating a revived Chinese nationalism. If Ahmadinejad remains in power as the president, he has to address the budget deficit brought about by plummeting oil prices and the world financial crisis and justify his administration's use of violence against those of his compatriots that he called "dust and dirt." Should street violence escalate in Iran, it also spells a turning point in Iran's domestic and foreign policies that the world will not forget or forgive. In short, no one can yet predict Iran's political future, but one thing is crystal clear. Even if the Iranian political establishment outlasts the current upheavals, unrest all over the country will play out over months and years to come. The Iranian system would settle down uncomfortably as a divided house. As such, even if authorities in Tehran undermine the popular and republican elements of the Iranian constitution, this would only increase their vulnerability to future democratic demands and to a legitimacy crisis that is hanging over their heads.

> "Ahmadinejad wants to retain the re-
> gime, but he wants to repopulate the
> leadership councils with clerics who
> share his populist values and want to
> revive the ascetic foundations of the re-
> gime."

The Iranian Government
Is Stable but Faces
Internal Division

George Friedman

*George Friedman asserts in the following viewpoint that the con-
troversial Iranian presidential elections in 2009 exposed the frac-
tures in that country's government. According to Friedman,
President Mahmoud Ahmadinejad has squared off against some
of the wealthy and powerful old-guard clergy that hold an interest in both the political and economic future of Iran. Though
some might think this internal conflict would pave the way for
liberalization, Friedman suggests that the resolution to this power
struggle is inconsequential because neither Ahmadinejad nor the
clergy wish to see an overturning of the state system. Therefore,
Friedman believes the current tension in Iran does not improve
chances for an Iranian democracy and does not signal the end of*

George Friedman, "The Real Struggle in Iran and Implications for U.S. Dialogue," Stratfor Global Intelligence, June 29, 2009. Reproduced by permission.

theocratic rule. Friedman is a political scientist and the founder of Stratfor Global Intelligence, a private intelligence corporation. Friedman also is the author of such works as America's Secret War, The Intelligence Edge, *and* The Future of War.

As you read, consider the following questions:

1. What is the "real struggle" in Iran, according to Friedman?

2. As Friedman states, President Ahmadinejad seeks to undermine Ayatollah Rafsanjani's power by calling into question what aspect of his life?

3. What are the two strategies that the Iranian government keeps in play to ensure regime survival, according to the author?

Speaking of the situation in Iran, U.S. President Barack Obama said June 26 [2009], "We don't yet know how any potential dialogue will have been affected until we see what has happened inside of Iran." On the surface that is a strange statement, since we know that with minor exceptions, the demonstrations in [Iran's capital] Tehran [after the June 12 elections] lost steam after Iranian Supreme Leader Ayatollah Ali Khamenei called for them to end and security forces asserted themselves. By the conventional wisdom, events in Iran represent an oppressive regime crushing a popular rising. If so, it is odd that the U.S. president would raise the question of what has happened in Iran.

In reality, Obama's point is well taken. This is because the real struggle in Iran has not yet been settled, nor was it ever about the liberalization of the regime. Rather, it has been about the role of the clergy—particularly the old-guard clergy—in Iranian life, and the future of particular personalities among this clergy.

Ahmadinejad Against the Clerical Elite

Iranian President Mahmoud Ahmadinejad ran his re-election campaign against the old clerical elite, charging them with corruption, luxurious living and running the state for their own benefit rather than that of the people. He particularly targeted Ali Akbar Hashemi Rafsanjani, an extremely senior leader, and his family. Indeed, during the demonstrations, Rafsanjani's daughter and four other relatives were arrested, held and then released a day later.

Rafsanjani represents the class of clergy that came to power in 1979 [after the Iranian Revolution]. He served as president from 1989–1997, but Ahmadinejad defeated him in 2005. Rafsanjani carries enormous clout within the system as head of the regime's two most powerful institutions—the Expediency Council, which arbitrates between the Guardian Council and parliament, and the Assembly of Experts, whose powers include oversight of the supreme leader. *Forbes* has called him one of the wealthiest men in the world. Rafsanjani, in other words, remains at the heart of the post-1979 Iranian establishment.

Ahmadinejad expressly ran his recent presidential campaign against Rafsanjani, using the latter's family's vast wealth to discredit Rafsanjani along with many of the senior clerics who dominate the Iranian political scene. It was not the regime as such that he opposed, but the individuals who currently dominate it. Ahmadinejad wants to retain the regime, but he wants to repopulate the leadership councils with clerics who share his populist values and want to revive the ascetic foundations of the regime. The Iranian president constantly contrasts his own modest lifestyle with the opulence of the current religious leadership.

Recognizing the threat Ahmadinejad represented to him personally and to the clerical class he belongs to, Rafsanjani fired back at Ahmadinejad, accusing him of having wrecked the economy. At his side were other powerful members of the regime, including Majlis Speaker Ali Larijani, who has made no secret of his antipathy toward Ahmadinejad and whose family links to the Shiite holy city of Qom give him substantial leverage. The underlying issue was about the kind of people who ought to be leading the clerical establishment. The battlefield was economic: Ahmadinejad's charges of financial corruption versus charges of economic mismanagement leveled by Rafsanjani and others.

When Ahmadinejad defeated Mir Hossein Mousavi on the night of the election, the clerical elite saw themselves in serious danger. The margin of victory Ahmadinejad claimed might have given him the political clout to challenge their position. Mousavi immediately claimed fraud, and Rafsanjani backed him up. Whatever the motives of those in the streets, the real action was a knife fight between Ahmadinejad and Rafsanjani. By the end of the week, Khamenei decided to end the situation. In essence, he tried to hold things together by ordering the demonstrations to halt while throwing a bone to Rafsanjani and Mousavi by extending a probe into the election irregularities and postponing a partial recount by five days.

The Struggle Within the Regime

The key to understanding the situation in Iran is realizing that the past weeks have seen not an uprising against the regime, but a struggle within the regime. Ahmadinejad is not part of the establishment, but rather has been struggling against it, accusing it of having betrayed the principles of the Islamic Revolution. The post-election unrest in Iran therefore was not a matter of a repressive regime suppressing liberals (as in Prague in 1989), but a struggle between two Islamist factions that are each committed to the regime, but opposed to each other.

The demonstrators certainly included Western-style liberalizing elements, but they also included adherents of senior clerics who wanted to block Ahmadinejad's re-election. And while Ahmadinejad undoubtedly committed electoral fraud to bulk up his numbers, his ability to commit unlimited fraud was blocked, because very powerful people looking for a chance to bring him down were arrayed against him.

The situation is even more complex because it is not simply a fight between Ahmadinejad and the clerics, but also a fight among the clerical elite regarding perks and privileges—and Ahmadinejad is himself being used within this infighting. The Iranian president's populism suits the interests of clerics who oppose Rafsanjani; Ahmadinejad is their battering ram. But as Ahmadinejad increases his power, he could turn on his patrons very quickly. In short, the political situation in Iran is extremely volatile, just not for the reason that the media portrayed.

Rafsanjani is an extraordinarily powerful figure in the establishment who clearly sees Ahmadinejad and his faction as a mortal threat. Ahmadinejad's ability to survive the unified opposition of the clergy, election or not, is not at all certain. But the problem is that there is no unified clergy. The supreme leader is clearly trying to find a new political balance while making it clear that public unrest will not be tolerated. Removing "public unrest" (i.e., demonstrations) from the tool kits of both sides may take away one of Rafsanjani's more effective tools. But ultimately, it actually could benefit him. Should the internal politics move against the Iranian president, it would be Ahmadinejad—who has a substantial public following—who would not be able to have his supporters take to the streets.

The View from the West

The question for the rest of the world is simple: Does it matter who wins this fight? We would argue that the policy differences between Ahmadinejad and Rafsanjani are minimal and probably would not affect Iran's foreign relations. This fight simply isn't about foreign policy.

Iran's Internal Division: Blessing or Curse?

The fight for political reform [in Iran] is intertwined with an entrenched factional struggle within the regime. Unlike 1979 [the Islamic revolution] when Iranians fought against a single, and undivided, political and military regime, Iran's current political elite is divided. Different armed groups back various conservative factions. The rift within the Islamic Republic may be a blessing for the democracy movement, a breathing space for regrouping, and moving forward. It may also be a recipe for an uncontrolled factional violence. The democracy movement may become collateral damage in a larger war. The future remains unclear.

Behzad Yaghmaian,
"Iran's Many Wars," Foreign Policy Journal,
June 25, 2009. www.foreignpolicyjournal.com.

Rafsanjani has frequently been held up in the West as a pragmatist who opposes Ahmadinejad's radicalism. Rafsanjani certainly opposes Ahmadinejad and is happy to portray the Iranian president as harmful to Iran, but it is hard to imagine significant shifts in foreign policy if Rafsanjani's faction came out on top. Khamenei has approved Iran's foreign policy under Ahmadinejad, and Khamenei works to maintain broad consensus on policies. Ahmadinejad's policies were vetted by Khamenei and the system that Rafsanjani is part of. It is possible that Rafsanjani secretly harbors different views, but if he does, anyone predicting what these might be is guessing.

Rafsanjani is a pragmatist in the sense that he systematically has accumulated power and wealth. He seems concerned about the Iranian economy, which is reasonable because he owns a lot of it. Ahmadinejad's entire charge against him is that Rafsanjani is only interested in his own economic well-being. These political charges notwithstanding, Rafsanjani was part of the 1979 revolution, as were Ahmadinejad and the rest of the political and clerical elite. It would be a massive mistake to think that any leadership elements have abandoned those principles.

When the West looks at Iran, two concerns are expressed. The first relates to the Iranian nuclear program, and the second relates to Iran's support for terrorists, particularly Hezbollah. Neither Iranian faction is liable to abandon either, because both make geopolitical sense for Iran and give it regional leverage.

Tehran's primary concern is regime survival, and this has two elements. The first is deterring an attack on Iran, while the second is extending Iran's reach so that such an attack could be countered. There are U.S. troops on both sides of the Islamic Republic, and the United States has expressed hostility to the regime. The Iranians are envisioning a worst-case scenario, assuming the worst possible U.S. intentions, and this will remain true no matter who runs the government.

We do not believe that Iran is close to obtaining a nuclear weapon, a point we have made frequently. Iran understands that the actual acquisition of a nuclear weapon would lead to immediate U.S. or Israeli attacks. Accordingly, Iran's ideal position is to be seen as developing nuclear weapons, but not close to having them. This gives Tehran a platform for bargaining without triggering Iran's destruction, a task at which it has proved sure-footed.

In addition, Iran has maintained capabilities in Iraq and Lebanon. Should the United States or Israel attack, Iran would thus be able to counter by doing everything possible to destabilize Iraq—bogging down U.S. forces there—while simultaneously using Hezbollah's global reach to carry out terror attacks. After all, Hezbollah is today's al Qaeda [terrorist organization responsible for September 11, 2001, attacks] on steroids. The radical Shiite group's ability, coupled with that of Iranian intelligence, is substantial.

Iran Will Not Be a Democracy Any Time Soon

We see no likelihood that any Iranian government would abandon this two-pronged strategy without substantial guarantees and concessions from the West. Those would have to include guarantees of noninterference in Iranian affairs. Obama, of course, has been aware of this bedrock condition, which is why he went out of his way before the election to assure Khamenei in a letter that the United States had no intention of interfering.

Though Iran did not hesitate to lash out at CNN's coverage of the protests, the Iranians know that the U.S. government doesn't control CNN's coverage. But Tehran takes a slightly different view of the BBC [British Broadcasting Corporation]. The Iranians saw the depiction of the demonstrations as a democratic uprising against a repressive regime as a deliberate attempt by British state-run media to inflame the situation. This allowed the Iranians to vigorously blame some foreigner for the unrest without making the United States the primary villain.

But these minor atmospherics aside, we would make three points. First, there was no democratic uprising of any significance in Iran. Second, there is a major political crisis within the Iranian political elite, the outcome of which probably tilts toward Ahmadinejad but remains uncertain. Third, there will be no change in the substance of Iran's foreign policy, regardless of the outcome of this fight. The fantasy of a democratic revolution overthrowing the Islamic Republic—and thus solving everyone's foreign policy problems a la the 1991 Soviet collapse—has passed.

That means that Obama, as the primary player in Iranian foreign affairs, must now define an Iran policy—particularly given Israeli Defense Minister Ehud Barak's meeting in Washington with U.S. Middle East envoy George Mitchell this Monday [June 29, 2009]. Obama has said that nothing that has happened in Iran makes dialogue impossible, but opening dialogue is easier said than done. The Republicans consistently have opposed an opening to Iran; now they are joined by Democrats, who oppose dialogue with nations they regard as human rights violators. Obama still has room for maneuver, but it is not clear where he thinks he is maneuvering. The Iranians have consistently rejected dialogue if it involves any preconditions. But given the events of the past weeks, and the perceptions about them that have now been locked into the public mind, Obama isn't going to be able to make many concessions.

It would appear to us that in this, as in many other things, Obama will be following the [George W.] Bush strategy—namely, criticizing Iran without actually doing anything about it. And so he goes to Moscow more aware than ever that Russia could cause the United States a great deal of pain if it proceeded with weapons transfers to Iran, a country locked in a political crisis and unlikely to emerge from it in a pleasant state of mind.

| "President Obama must make it crystal clear that the United States stands with the Iranian people, not with the repressive regime of the ayatollahs."

The U.S. Government Should Support Popular Opposition to the Iranian Election

James Phillips

In the following viewpoint, James Phillips demands that President Barack Obama's administration advocate for regime change in Iran by supporting the opposition movement and their quest for democracy. In Phillips's opinion, the administration has thus far avoided confrontation with the oppressive Iranian government. He believes, though, that in the wake of the brutal crackdown on demonstrators following the suspect presidential elections in June 2009, Obama should call for freedom in Iran by encouraging the global community to impose strict sanctions until the tyranny ends. Phillips is a senior research fellow for Middle Eastern affairs at the Heritage Foundation, a conservative public policy research institution.

As you read, consider the following questions:

1. Why does Phillips insist that a change in Iranian leadership during the 2009 presidential elections would have been meaningless?

2. Which western leader does Phillips say has taken the lead in speaking out against the oppressive Iranian regime?

3. As Phillips states, what has America received in return for its kid-glove approach to Iran?

The massive popular protests that have convulsed Iran [following the June 12, 2009 presidential election] have not only shattered the already weak claim to legitimacy of the radical regime in [Iran's capital] Tehran, but they have also undermined the [Barack] Obama Administration's strategy of diplomatically engaging that brutal dictatorship.

The regime has been vividly exposed as a ruthless tyranny willing to deceive, repress, and kill its own people—shattering any lingering doubts that some may have had as to its true nature. Consequently, the Obama Administration must recalibrate its Iran policy and take a tougher public stance in support of the Iranian opposition's campaign for greater freedom.

Engage the People, Not the Regime

The Administration undoubtedly hoped that bombastic President Mahmoud Ahmadinejad would be voted out of power and that a successor government would be easier to negotiate with on thorny issues such as Iran's nuclear program, support for terrorism, and threats against Israel.

But Ahmadinejad's chief presidential rival, former Prime Minister Mir Hossain Mousavi, is a leading member of Iran's revolutionary establishment who shares many of Ahmadinejad's goals—although he would pursue them in a less confrontational manner. On foreign policy issues, Mousavi would adopt a calmer tone but would remain committed to Iran's nuclear program, which began during his term as prime minister.

President Barack Obama has wisely not taken a position on the internal power struggle between Ahmadinejad and Mousavi, who may be Tweedledum and Tweedledee on many foreign policy issues that are a priority for the United States. But the President has not spoken out adequately in support of the Iranian people's struggle for freedom. Such advocacy is not meddling; it is an appropriate defense of basic human rights that are being trampled in Iran.

The election travesty should be a confirmation for the Administration that the only vote that counts today in Iran's Islamist system is the vote of the Supreme Leader, Ayatollah Ali Khamenei. While Iranian presidents come and go, the unelected Supreme Leader retains the final say on all important matters. The mass rejection of the official vote tally has destroyed the illusion, carefully nurtured by the regime, that Iran's government is a quasi-democracy.

In his inaugural speech, President Obama famously proclaimed, "To those who cling to power through corruption and deceit and the silencing of dissent, know that you are on the wrong side of history, but that we will extend a hand if you are willing to unclench your fist."

Now that it is clear that the regime's fist remains tightly clenched around the throat of the Iranian people, the Obama Administration cannot simply take a business-as-usual approach to Iran's clerical dictatorship.

The United States Must Stand for Freedom

President Obama should drop the guarded language that suggests he is triangulating between the regime and its opposition and come down off the fence and on to the side of those fighting for freedom and democracy in Iran. Oblique equivocations about the regime's strong-arm tactics and the killing

Time to Abandon Neutrality

The [U.S.] president needs to say to the world that we're choosing sides in this conflict and that we're rooting for the protesters against the people who are trying to beat them into submission and suppress the tides of progress.

He needs to abandon his neutrality and express clearly the principles that our country represents . . . and why we are moved by what we see happening in Iran. He needs to tell the protesters with all the sincerity he can muster: "We are with you!"

Ruben Navarrette Jr.,
"Obama Must Speak Out on Iran,"
CNN.com, June 19, 2009.

of at least seven unarmed demonstrators represent a moral myopia that in the long run undermines U.S. interests by signaling to the regime that its repressive violence comes at little cost to its own interests.

As the President has bent over backwards to avoid "meddling" in Iran's affairs, French President Nicolas Sarkozy has stepped up to fill the vacuum of leadership, placing the blame for the current crisis squarely on Iran's ruling regime. Meanwhile, Tehran has accused Washington [U.S. government] of meddling anyway.

Voicing support for Iranians struggling to reclaim their freedom promotes American ideals and universal human rights and advances American national interests. Ultimately, Tehran will cease to be a threat to its neighbors, Americans, and its own people when Iranians are free to pursue their own national interests rather than the narrowly defined interests of the radical regime.

President Obama must make it crystal clear that the United States stands with the Iranian people, not with the repressive regime of the ayatollahs [religious leaders]. He should strongly denounce the violent suppression of the democratic opposition and the systematic human rights abuses perpetrated by the regime. Moreover, he should call on other world leaders to cooperate in pressuring Tehran to end its persecution of political reformers, human rights activists, and religious minorities.

America Must Lead Global Opposition

Rather than abdicating leadership on the human rights issue in an unseemly attempt to strike a deal with the outlaw regime, President Obama should seize the moral high ground and rally international support for effective economic and political sanctions on Tehran. He should call on European and other allies to impose the same level of economic sanctions that the United States has imposed on Iran since 1995. Depriving Tehran of a vital source of foreign investment, trade, and loans would maximize pressure on the regime, which is unlikely to make concessions on the nuclear program or its treatment of its own citizens unless it is convinced that its hold on power is threatened.

Only strong international pressures that impose excruciating economic pain—not soothing rhetoric or misconceived attempts at appeasement—are likely to have an effect on the callous Iranian regime. But so far, the Obama Administration has treated the Tehran regime with kid gloves and received nothing in return except for religious lectures, an accelerating uranium enrichment program, and continued Iranian support for insurgents killing Americans and U.S. allies in Iraq and Afghanistan.

President Obama should speak truth to power and put America on the right side of history. He should no longer mute his Administration's criticism of a despicable regime in a vain effort to diplomatically assuage it. Otherwise, future American Presidents may have to apologize to the Iranian people for leaving them in the clenched fist of Iran's clerical dictatorship.

> "The idea that the occupant of the Oval Office must pass moral judgment on all events, including other countries' elections, is a byproduct of America's imperial pretensions and delusions of 'world leadership.'"

The U.S. Government Should Not Become Involved in the Iranian Election

Justin Raimondo

In the viewpoint that follows, Justin Raimondo notes how the disputed outcome of the 2009 presidential election in Iran has not prompted the White House to speak out against the probable injustice of the voting process. Instead, Raimondo claims that the U.S. government may be actively pursuing covert operations in Iran to destabilize Iran's theocratic regime. Pointing out that American elections are not always shining examples of democracy, Raimondo argues that U.S. politicians have no moral high ground from which to judge Iran's affairs. He asserts that America should learn to stay out of matters of foreign self-

Justin Raimondo, "Iran's Election: None of America's Business," Antiwar.com, June 14, 2009. Reproduced by permission.

determination and should end its imperial dream of world leadership. Raimondo is the editorial director and a columnist for Antiwar.com, a libertarian Web site espousing noninterventionist global policy.

As you read, consider the following questions:

1. What problems does Raimondo say Iranian President Mahmoud Ahmadinejad has brought upon his country?

2. According to the author, how will the Ahmadinejad government take advantage of any censure from the Obama administration concerning the 2009 elections?

3. How does Raimondo criticize the U.S. presidential election process?

Was it [political commentator] Daniel Pipes' endorsement of President Mahmoud Ahmadinejad that put the Holocaust-denying hard-liner over the top in Iran's recent presidential "election"? Or was it the massive—and fairly obvious—fraud committed by the Ahmadinejad camp?

Joking aside, at least for the moment, one has to wonder: what else did anybody expect? Iranian elections have hardly been models of democratic governance in the past. The supreme leader, Ayatollah Khamenei, prefigured the probable upshot of all this when he announced that a victory for leading opposition candidate Mir Hossein Mousavi would amount to a repudiation of him personally—and the crackdown we are witnessing could only have come about as a direct result of Khamenei's order.

The U.S. government—or, at least, one branch of it—didn't help matters much. Their fast-tracking of draconian new sanctions on Iran right before Iranians went to the polls could only have helped Ahmadinejad. How's that for timing?

In any case, the Mousavi challenge was a frontal assault on the legitimacy of the current regime, and they have responded just as tyrannical elites have always responded, with deadly force and brazen fraud.

The Hard-Liner Crackdown

Ahmadinejad has led his country into an economic dead end, with record unemployment, gas shortages, and a high inflation rate. That, combined with U.S. President Barack Obama's remarkable outreach to the Iranians—a video message of friendship, an offer to negotiate with Iranian leaders without preconditions, and an unprecedented acknowledgment of the U.S. government's role in overthrowing Mohammed Mossadegh's democratically elected government in 1953—would have sounded the death knell of the current gang if the election had been allowed to proceed unobstructed. As it was, the hard-liners sealed off Iran from the rest of the world as Mousavi's overwhelming victory became apparent, placed the candidate under house arrest (or so it seems from numerous unconfirmed news reports), shut down the Internet, and unleashed their "Revolutionary Guards" on student-led protest demonstrations.

The swiftness of the hard-liner response, however, can be deceiving. Apparently, there was confusion in the Ahmadinejad camp as Mousavi's victory loomed large. We are getting reports that the authorities informed Mousavi of his impending election victory before the polls had even closed, and he was advised to "moderate" his victory speech for fear of provoking a violent response from Ahmadinejad's supporters, many of whom are members of the "revolutionary" militias. The reformist newspapers, too, were told they were not allowed to use the word "victory" in reference to Mousavi when reporting election results—but at least they were allowed to report it. Or so they thought.

Shortly afterward, however, these same newspapers were taken over by armed assailants, Mousavi's election headquarters were surrounded by military forces under the hard-liners' command, and the regime's thugs were called out into the streets—where they met Mousavi's mostly youthful supporters in bloody clashes throughout the country.

Like [historian and political analyst] Juan Cole, I will readily admit that I may be wrong about the veracity of the hard-liner coup narrative, and I may very well have fallen for what some are calling the "North Tehran Fallacy"—the idea that Western reporters were lured into believing that Mousavi was the winner because they are all based in a relatively affluent and Westernized part of the Iranian capital [Tehran] (Cole, by the way, denies the validity of the North Tehran thesis, though it seems plausible to me.) Yet that really has no relevance to the main point of this column, which is this: America has no business intervening in Iran's internal affairs, including its presidential election. Period.

To do so would play right into the hands of Iran's hard-liners—and their neoconservative cheerleaders (both overt and covert) in this country. Whatever support the kooky Ahmadinejad had managed to garner—according to leaked and unconfirmed reports, about 30 percent of the total—was due almost entirely to external factors, principally the U.S.-led campaign to strangle the Iranian economy and rile up ethnic and religious minorities. This, in turn, has rebounded to the hard-liners' benefit, as anti-Americanism—long a staple of Iranian politics—has reached record levels throughout the region.

Overt Silence but Covert Action

So far, the Obama administration has kept its collective mouth shut pretty tight—except, of course, for [Vice President] Joe Biden—and that's a good thing. What isn't so good is that the White House will almost surely be forced to pronounce some sort of verdict or judgment on the apparently fraudulent election results. Criticism, however mild, coming from Washington [D.C.], will surely be used by Ahmadinejad & Co. as a pretext to declare a state of "emergency" and engineer a total crackdown. And the possibility of a dramatic showdown between the two Iranian camps is increasing by the moment:

Criticizing Iran's Elections Legitimizes the Regime's Claims of U.S. Interference

America must distance itself from discussions of sham elections—the American government's legitimacy to condemn stolen votes has not yet recovered from its own sham presidential elections of recent. It is actually not the place of the United States government to question the domestic elections of any nation—this is internal interference and it doesn't look good on the diplomatic or impartiality scales. It also further validates [President Mahmoud] Ahmadinejad's insistent claims of US plans for regime change. . . .

Overall, the United States must give the [Islamic] Republic [of Iran] less excuse for legitimacy in anyone's eyes.

Shirin Sadeghi,
"Post-Election Iran: What America Must Do Now,"
The Huffington Post, *June 14, 2009.*
www.huffingtonpost.com.

Mousavi is reportedly calling for his followers to take to the streets in protest—although there is some fear that this may be a trap set by the regime—and what follows may very well turn out to be an Iranian replay of what happened in China's Tiananmen Square, at least as far as the rest of the world sees it.

What this means, in terms of U.S. foreign policy, and the building "crisis" around U.S.-Iranian relations, is that the prospects for a negotiated settlement of the outstanding issues between the two countries have darkened considerably. Yes, I know Obama has declared his intention to soldier on in the "outreach" effort, but this will become increasingly untenable—and make it fairly easy for him to backtrack—as the authority and legitimacy of the Iranian government continues to deteriorate, as it will.

And we should not forget that, in spite of public assurances from the U.S. president that the administration wants peace, is prepared to negotiate, and that it's time for "a new beginning," the Americans continue their covert action operations directed at Tehran—as recent bombings and other disturbances in the eastern non-Persian provinces have shown. Is the U.S. involved in the current street fighting in Tehran and other major cities? I wouldn't be at all surprised to have this suspicion confirmed in coming days. After all, in 2007 Congress appropriated $400 million to destabilize the Iranian regime, and who's to say this program isn't bearing fruit?

America Has No Right to Pass Judgment on Iran

U.S. military leaders are vehemently opposed to launching yet another war in the Middle East, and their stubborn resistance to the idea—floated by [former President George W.] Bush's neocon camarilla in the latter days of the Decider's reign—scotched the War Party's attempts to make sure Obama inherited a Middle East aflame. Yet their efforts will have reached beyond the previous administration's grave—and succeeded in dragging Obama down with them into hell—if events in Iran provoke an ill-considered response from the U.S.

Whenever there are election "irregularities" anywhere outside the U.S., American government officials have a bad habit of getting up on their high horses and lecturing the rest of the world on how best to conduct their own internal affairs. Never mind that the U.S. itself has only two officially recognized political parties, both of which are subsidized with tax dollars, and that any potential rivals must jump through a number of hoops to even get on the ballot. We're a legend in our own minds—the world's greatest "democracy"—and anyone who questions this dubious claim is immediately charged with "anti-Americanism."

Yet even if that were not the case—even if our democratic procedures were flawless—that still wouldn't give the U.S. government any standing to pass judgment, because how Iran conducts its presidential elections is not a legitimate concern of the U.S. government. The idea that the occupant of the Oval Office must pass moral judgment on all events, including other countries' elections, is a byproduct of America's imperial pretensions and delusions of "world leadership."

The Israel lobby, which has been pushing for a U.S. confrontation with Iran, is revving up its engines even now to push harder for increased sanctions and other provocative moves by the U.S. Obama, I fear, will prove unable to resist all that pressure, though I'd love to be proven wrong.

Periodical Bibliography

The following articles have been selected to supplement the diverse views presented in this chapter.

Iason Athanasiadis and Barbara Slavin	"Crude Prisons Crop Up in Tehran during Crackdown on Protesters," *Washington Times*, July 31, 2009.
Economist	"Not over Yet: Iran's Shaky Government," September 19, 2009.
John P. Hannah	"Wake-Up Call: Time to Get Serious about Helping Iran's Opposition," *Weekly Standard*, September 9, 2009.
Amitabh Pal	"The Iranian Example," *Progressive*, August 2009.
Scott Peterson	"At Stake in Iran Uprising: Trust in the Islamic Revolution," *Christian Science Monitor*, June 21, 2009.
Michael Petrou	"'We Have Finally Learned to Fight': Iran's Regime Took the Election, but It Also Set the Stage for Radical Upheaval," *Maclean's*, June 29, 2009.
Laura Secor	"Protest Vote," *New Yorker*, June 29, 2009.
Amir Taheri	"Ahmadinejad's Last Stand? The Meaning of Iran's Upcoming Presidential Election," *National Review*, May 25, 2009.
Robert F. Worth	"Iran Expanding Effort to Stifle the Opposition," *New York Times*, November 24, 2009.

OPPOSING
VIEWPOINTS®
SERIES

CHAPTER 4

What Are the Current Problems in Iran?

Chapter Preface

When the Islamic Revolution swept aside the shah of Iran's government in 1979, the ruling clerical leaders assured their people and the world that Iranians would no longer suffer the abuses they had under the previous regime. Rigged elections and a general lack of political freedom were commonplace under the shah, who rooted out dissenters with his infamous secret police. The Ayatollah Ruhollah Khomeini, the supreme leader of Iran after the revolution, promised these practices would end with the downfall of the shah. However, human rights organizations have argued that during the reign of Khomeini and his successor, the Ayatollah Ali Khamenei, Iranians have not received their promised freedom. In its February 5, 2009, document "Iran: Human Rights in the Spotlight on the 30th Anniversary of the Islamic Revolution," Amnesty International, a human rights organization that has monitored Iran since the 1960s, claims that "impunity, arbitrary arrest, torture, and other ill-treatment, as well as the use of the death penalty remain prevalent" in post-revolution Iran.

Amnesty International states that the clerical regime has clamped down on freedom of expression—especially in the political arena—by forcibly closing newspapers and even Web sites for airing dissenting opinions. Those who choose to speak ill of the state religion are often flogged or imprisoned, the organization maintains. Amnesty International estimates that "hundreds, if not thousands, of people" are arrested each year in Iran under vague charges relating to offenses against the state. According to the monitors, many of these suspects are denied legal counsel to help refute any allegations.

Amnesty International also reports that the dreaded secret police force that worked so efficiently under the shah has been replaced by agents of capital city Tehran's Ministry of Intelligence, who find, detain, and sometimes torture suspects in the months it may take for the state's case to reach trial. Amnesty International contends that methods of interrogation used on detainees during such waiting periods have included "beatings, suspension from a height, insults, threat of rape, sexual abuse, electric shocks, prolonged sleep deprivation, being forced to stand in uncomfortable positions for long periods, and prolonged solitary confinement." The organization concludes that even if a suspect survives to trial, the legal proceedings often end with a summary judgment pronounced after a confession (extracted under torture) with little or no corroborating evidence.

Spokespersons for the Iranian government have continually refuted these claims of human rights abuse. Some have insisted that the United States is behind these trumped-up charges. They assert that the U.S. government refuses to see the vast improvements in Iran since the revolution and simply disseminates lies to destabilize the Islamic regime. In 2002, Foreign Ministry representative Hamid Reza Asefi pointed out that "the U.S. itself lacks an unblemished file concerning the establishment of equal conditions for all citizens of its own country and observing their rights." Citing ongoing discrimination against minorities, Asefi maintained in his rebuttal (reprinted in China's *People's Daily* newspaper) that "American shortsightedness in its obstinate accusation of other countries" constituted "unconventional diplomatic behavior." Forced to recognize that America does not make such accusations alone, the Iranian government has made similar rebuttals against the United Nations and other international organizations that question Iran's human rights progress.

Human rights violations have dogged Iran's efforts to integrate into the global community. In the chapter that follows, various authors examine additional problems that have impeded Iran's internal growth as well as complicated its relations with other countries.

| "Should oil prices fall significantly, the
Iranian regime could not easily cope."

The Iranian Government Is Crippling Iran's Economy

Patrick Clawson

In the following viewpoint, Patrick Clawson maintains that since the reign of the shah, Iran has fueled its economic growth on oil revenues. Clawson claims that, because of this focus, Iran has not diversified its economy. Furthermore, although oil has brought prosperity to some Iranians, Clawson states that the income has not been invested in changing Iran's infrastructure to improve the lives of all Iranians—especially those living farther away from the oil producing regions. Clawson observes that as oil prices fluctuate, Iran's fortunes also waver, and government price controls, subsidies, and other attempts to fix the marketplace are exacerbating the lack of stability in an economy tied to one commodity. Clawson is senior editor for Middle East Quarterly *and deputy director for research at the Washington Institute for Near East Policy.*

Patrick Clawson, "The Islamic Republic's Economic Failure," *Middle East Quarterly*, vol. xv, Fall 2008, pp. 15–26. Copyright © 2008 The Middle East Forum. Reproduced by permission.

As you read, consider the following questions:

1. How did the shah's emphasis on oil wealth help lead to the overthrow of his regime, according to Clawson?

2. As cited by Clawson, what percentage of unemployment does the International Monetary Fund predict Iran will suffer in 2010?

3. How is President Ahmadinejad trying to lower interest rates in Iran, and what does Clawson say has been the result of this strategy?

The Islamic Republic's nuclear drive remains a focal point of international concern. President Mahmoud Ahmadinejad speaks of becoming a pan-regional if not world power. Much of his defiance is fueled by unprecedented oil income. Iran has built a US$82 billion foreign exchange reserve. But behind Ahmadinejad's blustery confidence and defiance, decades-old systemic forces are eroding Iran's economic stability. Iran has suffered perhaps more than any Middle Eastern country from the "oil curse." As Iran became addicted to oil, it postponed reform and let the rest of its economy languish. While record oil prices insulate the Islamic Republic from the consequences of its leaders' decisions, any significant decline may force an internal reckoning.

The Shah Focuses on Oil Wealth

As the Islamic Revolution completes its third decade, it would be easy to blame all economic problems on its leadership. In reality, though, economic mismanagement has remained a constant during Iran's imperial and revolutionary eras.

Throughout the two decades between Prime Minister Mohammad Musaddiq's fall and the 1973 oil shock, oil exports accounted for more than 80 percent of Iranian foreign exchange income. Broadly speaking, without the revenue it earns from oil, the Iranian government would have been half its actual size. Iran used its oil income efficiently through 1972, funding reasonable development projects and social infrastructure. The proof is Iran's exemplary record of economic growth: In a 2004 report, the International Monetary Fund (IMF) concluded, "During 1960–76, Iran enjoyed one of the fastest growth rates in the world: The economy grew at an average rate of 9.8 percent in real terms, and real per capita income grew by 7 percent on average. As a result, GDP [gross domestic product] at constant prices was almost 5 times higher in 1976 than in 1960." Oil price increases do not affect these figures, which are adjusted for price increases.

Iran's oil output increased far beyond the pre-nationalization peak of 600,000 barrels per day (b/d). This expansion was driven by [Iran's ruler] the shah [Muhammed Reza Pahlavi], not by the consortium of international oil companies producing in Iran. The image promoted by Iranian nationalists and some historians that Musaddiq stood up to a shah who had obediently provided oil to the West is distorted; in reality, the shah spent twenty-five years pushing international oil companies hard to get more money for Iran. The concession he negotiated with the international oil companies after Musaddiq's overthrow was much more favorable to Iran than the pre-nationalization agreement, providing a 50-50 division of the profits. By 1960, revenue was more than eightfold above the 1950 level, a figure only partly due to a 50 percent increase in output. The National Iranian Oil Company (NIOC), founded in 1955, sought smaller oil companies willing to accept a 25–75 profit split in favor of Iran to develop fields outside the concession area, that is, the area over which the consortium of international oil companies had a monopoly. . . .

The Socio-Economic Scene

Iranians gave the shah little credit for Iran's booming economy and the accompanying rapid rise in income. Rather, the general mood of the time was one of unmet expectations. The shah had promised the Iranian people European-style income, and he could not deliver. In a 1974 interview, the shah promised, "In twenty-five years, Iran will be one of the world's five flourishing and prosperous nations . . . I think that in ten years' time, our country will be as you [in Britain] are now." The shah's forecast, which reinforced Iranians' self-conception of their country's natural greatness, exacerbated the expectation gap.

Part of the problem was that not everyone in society benefited equally from the prosperity. While the spending power of poor Iranians increased, so too did the gap between the poor and the upper class. There was also a huge geographic disparity; in 1971, average household expenditures in [the capital] Tehran were more than two and half times those in the impoverished southeastern province of Kerman. But the greater political problem for the shah was that economic modernization was not well accepted by Iranian intellectuals.

The dominant intellectual trend at the time was Third Worldism, a mix of socialism and anti-imperialism which blames the West, the United States, and the local elites who pursue harmonious relations with the West for the shortcomings of developing countries. In Iran, Third Worldism went beyond the usual neo-Marxism to assume a strong nativist character. One of the most influential books of the period was Jalal al-Ahmad's *Gharbzadegi* (Westoxication). Ahmad argued that Iranians risked abandoning their culture in favor of the West's, a eulogy for a passing era that melded Iranian nationalism with anti-Western discourse.

Too Much Growth Too Fast

The 1979 Islamic Revolution was not about the economy, but the economic situation certainly helped undermine the shah. After oil prices rose rapidly in 1973, the shah predicted the rapid transformation of Iran into an advanced industrial country, but Iranians watched as government mismanagement squandered much of the oil wealth. Paradoxically, the post-1973 flood of oil income slowed growth: Too much was attempted, and the resulting logjams stopped progress. In contrast to the preceding decade, the government badly mismanaged the economy after 1973. Government revenue from oil rose from $5 billion in 1973 to $19 billion the following year. In August 1974, one year into his fifth economic plan, the shah increased government spending from $44 billion to $123 billion. He pressed ahead full steam on every front, ignoring the serious constraints to implementing so many projects simultaneously and changing policy so frequently. The higher spending on everything from the military, to infrastructure investments, government salaries, and social welfare programs increased demand for goods and services to a level the domestic economy could not supply. Nor could Iran's transport system handle the ensuing demand for imports; in 1975, ships had to wait between 160 to 250 days to enter Iran's principal port, Khorramshahr, at the tip of the Persian Gulf. Tehran had to pay more than $1 billion in charges for ships stuck in ports unable to unload. The combination of high demand and tight supply led to a sharp increase in inflation to an average of 15 percent per year between 1973 and 1978, from an annual rate of less than 4 percent before. . . .

By late 1976, the economy was in bad shape, with national income growing only slowly while shortages of electricity, water, cement, and some foodstuffs constrained output and fed popular discontent. At last, the shah reversed course, acknowledging he had wrongly pushed too fast. He appointed a new prime minister who suspended many development projects and introduced an International Monetary Fund-style stabilization program in March 1978. The overheated economy began to cool and inflation abated. But the price of curtailed government spending was fewer new jobs and falling real incomes while the supply constraints caused shortages to persist. The economic constraints played no small part in feeding the political discontent that exploded in Iran's streets in 1978.

The Government Hijacks the Economy

The Islamic Revolution, of course, was about politics, not economics. Once the revolutionaries came to power, the Iranian economy deteriorated due to both quasi-socialist policies and the war with Iraq. Every time it looked like the revolutionaries would be forced to compromise their hard-line stances, oil income came to their rescue. By the time the Iran-Iraq war ended in 1988, average incomes had dropped by more than half. Grand hopes for postwar recovery floundered as entrenched revolutionaries, who benefited from the crazy-quilt of regulations, reasserted their power, and the government fell back on its old ways of muddling through on the strength of oil income.

The economy was not a priority for Ayatollah Ruhollah Khomeini. He quipped, "I do accept that any prudent individual can believe that the purpose of all these sacrifices was to have less expensive melons." Within just a few years, a Third Worldist group of clerics and bureaucrats espousing interventionist policies in the name of social justice triumphed over bazaar merchants, traditionalist clerics opposed on religious grounds to almost any state intervention, and Western-oriented technocrats. Faced with chaos in factories and a banking system close to collapse, the revolutionary government nationalized much of the economy and transferred assets of the former shah and his supporters to revolutionary foundations (*bonyads*). Only small industries remained in private hands.

Over time, the government's control over the economy increased. State-controlled prices dissuaded foreign investment, and the government regulated all economic activity through an unwieldy permit system. Mosques distributed ration coupons. Since the cost of rationed goods was well below market prices, farmers had little incentive to increase output. The manufacturing sector suffered from both price controls and shortages of foreign investment. Making a profit depended on manipulating complicated regulations. In this atmosphere of legal confusion and bureaucratic restriction, the companies that did best were those owned by the state or the *bonyads*. . . .

Oil Revenues Cannot Sustain Iran's Economy

Through much of the Islamic Republic's first two decades, vigorous political debate within the narrow limits set by the revolutionary authorities has resulted in several changes in government leadership while real power always remained in the hands of the revolutionaries overseeing the formal government structure. The surprising 1997 landslide presidential election of reformist Mohammad Khatami inaugurated a short period when widespread reforms appeared inevitable. Then came the conservative reassertion, with violent repression and engineered elections spearheaded by the supreme leader and Revolutionary Guard veterans, leading eventually to the 2005 triumph of Mahmoud Ahmadinejad. Through all these maneuverings, inappropriate economic policies have been constant. The Iranian government wastes billions each year on subsidies and inefficient capital-intensive industries while small businesses drown in red tape and millions of young people face unemployment or underemployment.

If Khatami had well-formed and articulate social and political views, he had no comparable economic expertise. His long-awaited August 1998 Economic Rehabilitation Plan was blunt in its description of problems but modest in its proposals, and his third five-year-plan, announced the following year, was no different. Different political factions agreed that the economy was in bad shape and that drastic changes were needed, but no one was willing to tackle the entrenched interests that supported subsidies for consumer goods, which drained public coffers, or rampant corruption, which scared off foreign investors.

Failure to make headway on economic reform led to lackluster performance between 2000 and 2004. When the third economic plan was drafted in 1998, Iran's oil and gas exports were at their lowest level since the Iran-Iraq war, totaling only $9.9 billion for the year. As oil prices rose sharply, Iran's oil and gas exports shot up to $36.8 billion during the plan's last year. As Arab states such as the United Arab Emirates, Qatar, and Kuwait diversified their economies and investments to become less dependant on oil revenue or at least built up financial reserves abroad to cushion their economies in the event of a downturn in oil revenue, the Iranian government grew more reliant on oil revenues, which, by 2004, provided 64 percent of the government's income without calculating massive, implicit subsidies from cheap energy. . . .

In 2006, the IMF published a pessimistic assessment of Iran's economic prospects even if world oil prices remained around $65 per barrel. The organization predicted that between 2007 and 2011, inflation would remain at 17 percent a year, the government budget would slip into considerable deficit, and the unemployment rate would gradually increase from 11 percent in 2005 to 13.2 percent in 2010. The Iranian government's estimate that the labor force is growing by 700,000 per year almost certainly understates the number of people who would like to work since many young women no longer even bother to look for jobs.

Skyrocketing oil prices have far exceeded IMF forecasts. The Islamic Republic's oil and gas exports between March 2007 and March 2008 were higher than the combined total for all four years of the first Khatami term. Despite this windfall, economic conditions have deteriorated far beyond the IMF forecast. In mid-2008, Iran's Statistics Center estimated unemployment at 11.9 percent with the rate for those aged 15 to 24 reaching 25.6 percent. Were oil prices to fall, the situation would be grim. Should oil prices fall significantly, the Iranian regime could not easily cope.

Unbalancing the Economy

Insofar as Tehran's dependence on high oil prices distorts the economy, Ahmadinejad's administration has made it even more vulnerable. The Iranian president has exacerbated the worst aspects of past economic policies: He has expanded price controls, increased subsidies, and tied bank credits more to political factors than to business considerations.

He has implemented some economic reforms but only halfheartedly. Consider the long-debated move to ration energy supplies, a policy recommended by Iranian economists and their World Bank colleagues because of the lack of political will to raise energy prices to their actual cost. Rationing began in June 2007 but has been steadily undermined by periodic announcements of extra rations for populist reasons, such as summer and New Year's vacations. In addition to the monthly 26-gallon ration at $.48 per gallon, motorists can purchase extra amounts at $1.91 per gallon. While these measures may have slowed the growth of gasoline consumption, the total amount of gasoline sold in Iran in March 2008 was, at 618,300 barrels per day, above the 566,000 b/d pre-rationing level—hardly surprising given that the Islamic Republic is proudly pushing automobile production. With Iran's refineries uninterested in producing gasoline for which they receive such meager prices, the Iranian government has been forced to rely on imports. While these have oscillated, in 2006, for example, they amounted to 192,000 barrels per day. Those imports have become harder to obtain as Western banks have stopped offering letters of credit; two major suppliers—Reliance of India and Vitol of Switzerland—quit the Iranian market in 2007.

Continuing energy subsidies cost Iran $45 billion a year, according to former Central Bank governor Mohammed

Printing More Money Is Causing More Problems

Because it controls the oil revenue, which comes in U.S. dollars, [Iran] has a vested interest in a weak national currency. (It could get more rials [currency of Iran] for the same amount of dollars in the domestic market.) Mr. [President Mahmoud] Ahmadinejad has tried to exploit that opportunity by printing an unprecedented quantity of rials. Economists in Tehran speak of "the torrent of worthless rials" that Mr. Ahmadinejad has used to finance his extravagant promises of poverty eradication. The result has been massive flights of capital, mostly into banks in Dubai, Malaysia and Austria. Ayatollah Mahmoud Shahroudi, the Islamic Chief Justice, claims that as much as $300 billion may have left the country since President Ahmadinejad was sworn in.

Amir Taheri,
"Iran's Economic Crisis,"
Wall Street Journal, *May 9, 2007.*

Hossein Adeli. But even with that expenditure, the Islamic Republic cannot guarantee its citizens a secure energy supply. Natural gas consumption, on which most Iranians depend for heating and cooking, continues to be highly subsidized with the result that consumption is booming, forcing Iran to import more gas than it exports even though Iran has the world's second largest reserves. The government has difficulty paying for imports. When Turkmenistan cut off supplies in the midst of one of the coldest spells of weather Iran had experienced in decades in order to pressure Tehran to pay higher prices, the Iranian government had to shut off gas supplies to at least 1.4 million people.

Ahmadinejad's Denial and Deception

The real state of Iran's economy is becoming harder to judge as economic data becomes increasingly untrustworthy; for instance, Ahmadinejad's first minister of industry and mining, Eshaq Jahangari, reported that Ahmadinejad once ordered him to falsely double the reported economic growth rate. Ahmadinejad's 2008 budget was devoid of the detail that normally accompanies such documents. In order to make up shortfalls, the Ahmadinejad government has repeatedly raided the Oil Stabilization Fund, meant to accumulate a reserve when prices are high, as at present, for use when prices drop. Despite statutory provisions dictating that it is to receive the excess between the budget's estimated oil income (traditionally set conservatively) and actual revenue, the fund's balance actually decreased between March 2006 and December 2007, a period for which the fund should have received tens of billions of dollars. Annoyed at the few constraints he faced in such raids, Ahmadinejad simply dissolved the board charged with administering the fund.

Ahmadinejad often denies that standard economic principles apply to Iran. The most acute controversy has been about inflation. To the chagrin of many Iranian economists, the president denies that increasing the money supply 40 percent a year contributes to inflation. His anti-inflation policy centers on lowering the interest rate, first to 12 percent and then to 10 percent for most loans with his goal being to bring it into the single digits; sometimes he speaks about eliminating interest altogether on most bank loans. He has fired several top officials including two Central Bank governors and an economy minister for opposing this policy. Not surprisingly, its application has resulted in demand for loans that vastly exceeds supply, meaning that the only people who can get loans are the politically well-connected. By the government's own accounting, inflation has increased to 24 percent although many observers think the figure an understatement. Iran has been hit especially hard by the worldwide increase in food prices, particularly for wheat and rice, which are staples of the Iranian diet.

With price controls, loans hard to come by, and oil income allowing a flood of imports, production inside Iran is unattractive. With nowhere else to put their money, Iranian investors have speculated in real estate, a phenomenon that has widened the gap between poor and rich into a chasm. Mid-level bureaucrats or high school teachers might make a monthly salary of $300, but upscale apartments in Tehran sell for $600–$1,000 per square foot. One 15,000 square foot apartment in Tehran recently sold for $21 million. A whole industry has arisen to furnish the palaces of the nouveau riche. This mix of developments—huge profits for the wealthy and unprecedented oil income on the one hand, and rising unemployment and soaring inflation on the other—is politically explosive.

Western Pressure Adds to the Problems

While Ahmadinejad grabs headlines in Iran for his economic policies, real power on the issue rests with the supreme leader, Ali Khamenei, who has only fitful interest in the problem. While he makes sensible general statements from time to time, during his presidency (1981–89) he consistently advocated the same kind of oil-centered, statist, populist policies that Ahmadinejad now implements. Khamenei appears skeptical of any economic reform proposals. His hatred of the West may contribute to his distrust of economic reform, perhaps, because he sees basic economic principles as Western. He speaks often with evident passion about his conviction that the Islamic Republic is deeply threatened by Western cultural invasion, which could overthrow the regime as quickly as the Eastern European communist regimes fell.

As the nuclear confrontation between the West and Iran has accelerated, the U.S. government has developed an effective program of "informal sanctions" to press banks around the world to restrict or cut ties with Iran. By emphasizing the shady transactions in which Iranian banks have engaged, the U.S. Treasury Department has persuaded several important banks to withdraw from Iran; the number of foreign branches operating in Iran dropped from twenty-six in 2006 to twenty in 2008. In February 2008, the 32-nation Financial Action Task Force—the major body monitoring money laundering for illicit activities—warned of Tehran's "deficiencies" at preventing money laundering for terrorism and weapons of mass destruction development and called on banks to exercise "due diligence" when dealing with the Islamic Republic. Iranian officials complained that not only European but also Chinese banks cut their activities in Iran. Denied bank services, Iranian traders had to carry suitcases of cash to pay for imports.

International sanctions have also played a part even if the need for international consensus watered them down significantly. The U.N. [United Nations] Security Council adopted three resolutions placing restrictions on financial transactions for Iran's nuclear or missile programs, including banning transactions with one bank and urging diligence about other financial dealings. The Security Council resolutions also ordered tight limits on the export of "dual use" goods that could benefit Iran's nuclear or missile programs, some of which also have important civilian uses.

Iran's Success Depends on Foreign Investment

The European Union imposed further restrictions, which some European countries implemented with vigor. The effect has been to make Iran a less desirable market for European firms. For instance, German exports to Iran have fallen sharply in recent years while export credits backed by the German government were only 20 percent of the 2004 level in 2007. While there is no reliable estimate of how such financial sanctions have hit Iran, it would be safe to say that their direct cost is in the billions of dollars a year, and they have made the Islamic Republic even less attractive as a business destination.

Both because of Tehran's own internal economic difficulties and its political radioactivity, few foreign industrial firms have sought to locate inside Iran, other than Renault, which built a large automobile assembly plant. Not even its oil and gas reserves have tempted foreign companies to invest significantly in Iran. British and French government pressure reportedly led Shell and Total to postpone development of a large natural gas project; Japanese firms backed off from the large Azadegan oil and gas field development for the same reasons. That creates a real problem for Iran's oil-centered economic development model. Each year, Iran's oil fields produce 500,000 barrels per day less oil, according to Iran's oil minister. Iran's National Oil Company has used domestic financing and expertise to mitigate this decline, but Iran has made painfully slow progress at realizing its 20-year-old ambition to raise production capacity to 6 million barrels per day. Indeed, capacity is substantially lower than it was thirty years ago. While Iranian firms are developing Azadegan on their own, they are proceeding at a fraction of the hoped-for pace with foreign partners. The same is true of other major oil and gas projects, such as the construction of Iran's first liquefied natural gas facility to export gas by ship.

Ahmadinejad's attitude seems to be similar to that of his predecessors: that, at the end of the day, Iran's ample oil and gas reserves will make up for any shortcomings. And to be sure, the oil income increase of recent years is arguably the single most important reason Iran has been able to carry on its aggressive foreign policy, confront the international community about its nuclear program, and boldly support anti-American forces across the Middle East if not the world.

> "U.S. sanctions have targeted Iran's most vulnerable sectors, and the power of the United States is such that it can do great damage even with only limited support from others."

International Sanctions Are Crippling Iran's Economy

William R. Hawkins

William R. Hawkins argues in the following viewpoint that U.S. sanctions against Iran are crippling its economy. As Hawkins explains, without access to U.S. investment capital, Iran has been unable to expand its petroleum reserves, the main source of Iranian income. In addition, because the United States has closed off financial aid, other foreign nations have withheld their capital, fearing that Iran is too great a risk for investment. Hawkins stipulates that Iran must change its foreign policy and give up its nuclear ambitions and support of terrorism in order to end the sanctions. Hawkins is a senior fellow for national security studies at the U.S. Business and Industry Council in Washington, D.C.

William R. Hawkins, "Iran's Unrest Shows Power of Economic Sanctions," *Family Security Matters*, June 26, 2009. Reproduced by permission. www.FamilySecurityMatters.org.

As you read, consider the following questions:

1. What must Iran do to escape its "stagflation trap," in Hawkins's view?

2. According to the author, what prompted President Ronald Reagan to institute an embargo on Iran in 1987?

3. What does Hawkins see as the weaknesses of President Barack Obama's "open hand" policy?

Iran's Supreme Leader Ayatollah Ali Khamenei and the theocratic Guardian Council continue their violent suppression of those protesting the re-election of President Mahmoud Ahmadinejad in a vote that looks to have been rigged on a massive scale [in June 2009]. Pro-democracy demonstrators have suffered hundreds of casualties as security forces have swept them from the streets. "Those arrested in recent events will be dealt with in a way that will teach them a lesson," said Ibrahim Raisi, a judiciary official.

The central issue in the election was the deteriorating state of the Iranian economy which is hurting the middle class and limiting the opportunities of the country's rising generation. Many commentators have claimed that because of the domestic focus of the political campaign, there is no connection to the foreign policy issues that darken U.S.-Iran relations. Such an interpretation fails to understand that Iran's behavior in world affairs has carried a high price in the form of sanctions that have hit key sectors of the economy quite hard.

Iran's Floundering Economy

Economic sanctions are most commonly thought [of] as a way to pressure foreign governments to refrain from behavior at odds with American interests. Where, however, a regime is determined to follow an adversarial course of action—as has been the case in Iran where a militant dictatorship pursues policies based on religious zeal, the aim of sanctions is to weaken the ability of the rogue rulers to act by denying them the material and financial resources they need to support their ambitions. In the long run, it is hoped that the pain felt by the general population from the hardship imposed by sanctions will discredit the regime. Economic failure can lead to unrest, even revolution, as people come to understand that their standard of living is being adversely affected by the dangerous actions of their nation's leaders. This appears to be happening in Iran.

According to the most recent (August 2008) country report prepared by the International Monetary Fund [IMF], unemployment is Iran is expected to stay above 10 percent for the foreseeable future. It is currently estimated to be around 17 percent. Every year, 800,000 new people enter the labor market, but only half that many jobs are created. To stimulate the economy, the government has resorted to monetary and fiscal policies that have done more to generate inflation than jobs. The IMF expects inflation to remain around 25 percent per year.

Iran is caught in a stagflation trap it cannot escape unless it improves its business climate, reduces investment risk, loosens the regulatory grip of the mullahs [religious leaders], and regains access to international capital and technology. It cannot do these things until it changes its aggressive foreign policy that is threatening regional and global stability. Its restless population, yearning to advance, must realize that their lives cannot improve until Iran abandons its nuclear program and stops spreading terrorism.

The Power of U.S. Sanctions

The United States has imposed an array of economic sanctions on Iran. Often it is said that unilateral sanctions are ineffective, and certainly the impact of American sanctions has been weakened by Iranian trade with Europe, Russia and China. Multilateral sanctions imposed by the United Nations

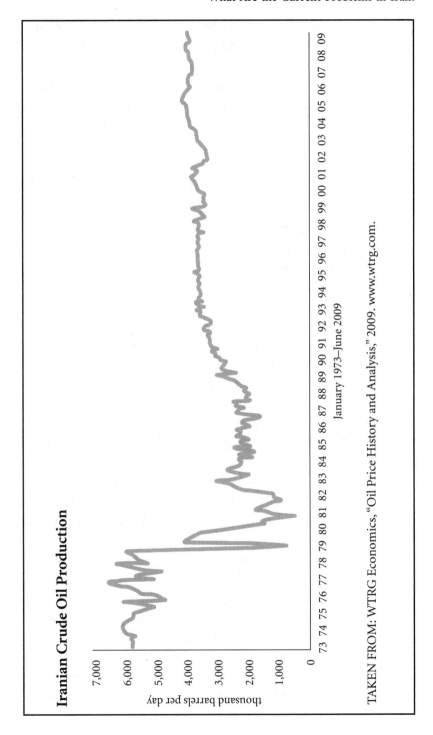

Iranian Crude Oil Production

thousand barrels per day

January 1973–June 2009

TAKEN FROM: WTRG Economics, "Oil Price History and Analysis," 2009. www.wtrg.com.

[UN] Security Council have been watered down by Russia and China. Yet, U.S. sanctions have targeted Iran's most vulnerable sectors, and the power of the United States is such that it can do great damage even with only limited support from others. As the IMF report states, "Intensified international pressures on Iran have negatively affected economic activity. UN and U.S. sanctions against certain Iranian institutions have created difficulties for trade financing and payments, discouraged foreign investment, and adversely affected the profitability of the targeted financial institutions."

As a result of Iran's support for international terrorism and its aggressive actions against shipping in the Persian Gulf during the Iran-Iraq War, President Ronald Reagan issued an executive order imposing a new import embargo on Iranian goods and services on October 29, 1987. Though there have been some modifications of this embargo in the years since (the [Bill] Clinton administration relaxed the trade sanctions in 2000 to allow the import of carpets and food products such as dried fruits, nuts, and caviar), the effect has been to prevent Iran from using exports to diversify its economy by expanding industries outside the oil sector. Iranian growth has not only been stunted, but the country has been kept more vulnerable because of its dependence on trade in one commodity.

In 1995, President Bill Clinton issued an executive order prohibiting U.S. involvement with petroleum development in Iran. And in 1997, he issued another order confirming that virtually all trade and investment activities with Iran by U.S. persons, wherever located, are prohibited. As the IMF reported, "Iran is endowed with vast hydrocarbon resources, but its capacity to increase hydrocarbon production is limited. In 2006, Iran had the second largest proven oil and gas reserves, and it was the fourth largest oil producer in the world. However, its oil production has remained virtually flat in recent years and will most likely stagnate in the medium term due to insufficient investment." U.S. sanctions are meant to deny Iran that investment.

[Iranian capital] Tehran's state oil firm estimates annual investment needs at $25–30 billion in the oil and gas sector. Iran plans to issue $12.3 billion worth of foreign currency and rial-denominated bonds over the next three years to help finance development of its huge South Pars gas field. But with American capital markets closed, and other foreign investors on edge due to the high level of tension in the area, Iran will have trouble raising such sums. One area Iran needs to expand is its petroleum refining capacity. Despite its large oil reserves, it still has to import gasoline. In a crisis, the U.S. could blockade Iran, cutting off both its oil exports and gasoline imports. Even without military action, the imposition of new sanctions to penalize companies that sell, ship, finance or insure refined petrol exports to Iran would breed further unrest as gasoline became scarce.

U.S. prohibitions on doing business with Iran's banking and financial sector cripples the ability of the regime to trade or attract capital. The regime knows that to improve its economic performance, it needs to reduce deficit spending, privatize state-owned industry, and curtail inflationary money creation. But it cannot make these reforms without finding other sources of capital and markets to take the place of government spending. And as long as its foreign policy behavior isolates it, it cannot find those sources. Indeed, the theocratic state has taken more direct control of the Central Bank to keep the money flowing because its priority is still spreading militancy in the region. Its nuclear ambitions and proxy armies in Lebanon and Gaza are more important to it than the economic progress of the Iranian people.

Iran Must Change Its Foreign Policy

Presidential contender Mir Hossein Mousavi wanted to reverse many of Iran's destructive economic policies. Many, including President Barack Obama, questioned whether in foreign policy Mousavi and Ahmadinejad were much different in outlook.

But Mousavi could not change the Iran economy without changing its foreign policy, as long as the United States holds its ground and maintains sanctions.

The danger is that the Obama administration will lift sanctions in the spirit of "engagement," allowing the theocratic regime to reduce domestic discontent without giving up its foreign ambitions. In his response to President Obama's "open hand" speech in March [2009], Supreme Leader Khamenei asked, "Have you released Iranian assets? Have you lifted oppressive sanctions? Have you given up mudslinging and making accusations against the great Iranian nation and its officials?" That Khamenei gave first priority to the removal of American sanctions indicates that they are a source of real pain to the regime.

To his credit, President Obama on March 12th extended existing sanctions on Iran due to the "unusual and extraordinary threat to U.S. national security" that Tehran poses. Unfortunately, the extension was only for one year, implying Obama hopes that relations might improve in the near future through his diplomatic initiative. Yet, the president has also said that if Iran continues its aggressive policies, additional "crushing" sanctions could be imposed.

At his June 23rd press conference, Obama still tried to cling to his "open hand" policy towards Iran, saying, "We have provided a path whereby Iran can reach out to the international community, engage, and become a part of international norms. It is up to them to make a decision as to whether they choose that path." The decision not to change the path they are on has been shown in Tehran as the regime's agents defend the fraudulent election results with force so as to stay in power. Therefore, the United States cannot afford to change its course either.

Economic sanctions must be increased to deny the Iranian theocracy the resources it needs to further its ambitions, and to convince the Iranian people that its leaders cannot provide them with the material progress they crave. The message must be clear: confronting the United States leads only to isolation and failure.

> "As women's rights activists increased their demands for equal rights and voiced their opposition to policies that worked against women, the crackdown on women's rights activists . . . increased proportionately."

The Iranian Government Has Impeded the Advancement of Women's Rights

International Campaign for Human Rights in Iran

In the following viewpoint, the International Campaign for Human Rights in Iran describes how the government under President Mahmoud Ahmadinejad has undermined the advances in women's rights made under the previous regime. As the organization claims, the Ahmadinejad administration has enforced strict dress codes for women, passed legislation that denigrates the power of women in marriage, set quotas on the number of women who can pursue university education, and banned women's advocacy groups that resist these measures. In addition, the organization asserts that the government routinely orders police to beat and jail protestors who speak out against this type of

"The Systematic Repression of the Women's Rights Movement—May 2008," International Campaign for Human Rights in Iran, January 14, 2009. Reproduced by permission.

oppression. The International Campaign for Human Rights in Iran is an advocacy group that monitors and reports on human rights violations.

As you read, consider the following questions:

1. What is the One Million Signatures Campaign, as the International Campaign for Human Rights in Iran describes it?

2. What was the university acceptance rate for women prior to the implementation of the government's quota system, according to the campaign?

3. How many members of the One Million Signatures Campaign have been arrested as of May 2008 for violations relating to their peaceful protests, as cited in the viewpoint?

The Iranian women's movement is the most vibrant social movement in Iran today. Despite repressive policies aimed at women and women's rights activists adopted by the government of President [Mahmoud] Ahmadinejad, women's rights activists have been able to articulate their message of legal reform, take it to the public, and influence discourse on women's rights at the highest levels of political decision-making. Much of the power and effectiveness of the women's movement today can be attributed to liberal policies adopted during the reform period and the Presidency of Mohammad Khatami [1997–2005]. Khatami, who was elected on a platform of promoting civil society, eased restrictions on the establishment of nongovernmental organizations (NGOs), and adopted policies specifically promoting the establishment of NGOs aiming to empower women and address the problem of honoring and implementing women's rights.

By the end of the reform period, and according to statistics provided by the Office of Women's Participation, over 600 women's NGOs had been established and registered. At the same time, the reformist government adopted policies and programs designed to strengthen the effectiveness of women's NGOs and promote networking. The government provided financial assistance for the establishment of women's NGOs and the implementation of their programs, and, indirectly, provided an opportunity for women's active social participation through civil society organizations.

According to one women's rights activist, who wished to remain anonymous:

> While these programs did little to directly empower those who are involved and in some way leading the women's movement today, the atmosphere of the time allowed for women's rights activists to set up organizations—many for the first time—and while working to empower women and meet their needs, these women's rights activists also became empowered in addressing social issues, found an opportunity to collaborate with one another, and learn about and identify the real priorities of Iranian women. As such, the reform movement and the opening up of social space facilitated greatly opportunities for women's rights activists, many of whom in the past had limited their activities to writing about women's issues, to test their capacities in social realm, and to learn how to work collaboratively.

According to another women's rights activist, awarding the Nobel Peace Prize to [Iranian lawyer and human rights activist] Shirin Ebadi [in 2003] also invigorated women's rights activists:

> For the first time, it seemed that the world was watching women's rights activists and civil society in Iran, and we felt at the time that we should come together to work collaboratively to address women's issues on a broader scale. We came together in the form of a Forum, or Hamanidishi Zanan, where women's rights activists met regularly to discuss issues of importance to women and approaches toward devising joint strategies for addressing women's concerns.

Activists Take to the Streets

This collaboration, which began in 2004, led to a protest in front of Tehran University in June 2005 objecting to laws that discriminate against women. The demand of the protesters to change discriminatory laws against women was the result of over a year of discussions among this group, who agreed that the most pressing issue facing and limiting women was indeed legal discrimination. Changing laws that place limits on women and discriminate against them was also the most common issue of concern for women's rights activists from different political and ideological backgrounds. Given that the protest was planned in the weeks leading up to the Presidential elections, and the relatively open social atmosphere of the time facilitated by the election atmosphere and Khatami's Reform Movement, the protesters—while facing some resistance by security forces—were tolerated. But while this protest was a major unifying event for the women's rights activists and NGOs who organized it, little was done to follow-up its demands in the year that followed. . . .

In June 2006, on the anniversary of the protest in front of Tehran University, another protest was planned in Hafte Tir Square in Tehran [Iran's capital city]. The organizers of the protest expected that security and police officials would use violence to disperse the crowd, and issued several statements in advance emphasizing the peaceful nature of the protest and its emphasis on the reform of laws that discriminate against women, focused this time primarily on family law. But the protest indeed ended in violence when police officers beat women protesters and more than 70 protesters were arrested. The majority of those arrested were released within the following week. This was the first time female police were used in a public assignment. The use of female police to beat and violently attack peaceful protesters was widely criticized by political observers and commentators as well as women's rights activists who had for years advocated for the establishment of a female police force in the hopes that women's issues would be dealt with more sensitively and appropriately. The violence used against protesters, the widespread arrest of equal rights defenders, and the security charges launched against protesters and organizers marked the first major crackdown against women's rights activists in Iran. But women's rights activists who had planned the protest were not deterred by this crackdown and instead devised a new plan to get to their message of equal rights to the public and law-makers. They started the One Million Signatures Campaign.

The One Million Signatures Campaign is seeking to reform discriminatory laws against women. Activists are asking for equal rights for women in marriage; equal rights to divorce for women; an end to the practice of polygamy and temporary marriage; an increase of the age of criminal responsibility to 18 for both girls and boys (currently 9 for girls and 15 for boys); the right for women to pass on nationality to their children; equal dieh (compensation for bodily injury or death) between women and men; equal inheritance rights; the reform of laws that reduce punishment for offenders in cases of honor killings; equal testimony rights for men and women in court; and to remove other laws that discriminate against women, including stoning sentences issued in cases of adultery. . . .

The Government Restricts Women's Rights

The Ahmadinejad presidency initiated several major policies to limit women's presence in the social sphere. Three of the most notable, upon which women's rights activists have focused their attention and criticism, include:

Program for Social Safety. The Program for Social Safety, which includes several components for combating immorality and criminality, was officially launched in March 2007. The first and most visible component of this program included combating inappropriate dress. The program, which has been

The Lot of Women Has Not Improved Under the Islamic Republic

The story of women's rights in Iran is one of advances and setbacks, stretching back to the start of the twentieth century, when a national women's movement first took shape. In the nineteen-thirties, the wearing of the traditional veil was banned, as Reza Shah sought to establish a modern secular state, and women were allowed into universities. During the reign of his son, women gained the right to vote and to enter parliament, and many became students and teachers. After the 1979 Revolution, many women's rights were taken away, and strict clothing laws were enforced. Today, the Islamic Republic's gender laws are among the harshest in the world. They penalize women in the areas of marriage, divorce, child custody, and inheritance. Polygamy is legal for men, and the legal testimony of one man carries the same weight as that of two women, an imbalance that helps explain why there are so few convicted rapists in Iran. Against this background, women . . . —[many of whom are] educated, cosmopolitan, and old enough to have come of age before the Islamic Revolution—occupy an anomalous position. They were formed in a society far more liberal, if not necessarily freer, than the one they now inhabit. And though Iranian women remain very highly educated by the standards of surrounding countries, the social and professional avenues open to them are often disappointingly narrow.

Francesco Bongiorni, "Veiled Threat,"
New Yorker, *October 5, 2009.*

carried out by special Guidance Police, includes identification of women whose appearance allegedly does not conform to appropriate Islamic dress and their subsequent arrest and detention. Special Guidance Police vans are usually placed strategically in busy squares. The officials identify women with bad hejab (Islamic covering) and load them into the vans, transferring them to local detention centers or offices of Amaken (in charge of monitoring immoral behavior in public places) where they are held until a family member can bring them appropriate clothing. These women are given a warning and are asked to enter into a signed agreement not to dress inappropriately in public again. Repeat offenders are referred to courts where fines and even lashings are issued as sentences. Women's rights defenders have objected to the Program for Social Safety on the grounds that it actually robs women of a sense of safety, is intended to restrict women's presence in public spaces, and is arbitrary: while observance of Islamic dress is the law, there is no standard within the law, and arresting officers are left free to judge whether a woman meets the standard or not. These arrests have apparently disproportionately targeted younger Iranians. Thousands of women have been detained through this program.

The Family Protection Act. Originally intended to streamline family legislation and court proceedings, this Act, submitted to the Parliament by the Judiciary in August 2007, included several provisions that women's rights activists found problematic. These provisions, it was later revealed, were included unconventionally, by the Executive Branch. The provisions that aroused the objections of women's rights activists and even reformist and some conservative political women included: 1) a provision that would allow men to take on a second wife, without obtaining an agreement from the first wife, and through court approval based solely on his financial ability to support more than one family; 2) a provision that would facilitate temporary marriage—the details of which were to be worked out by officials at a later date; 3) a provision that would set a standard rate for Mehrieh [dowry paid to a bride] and would impose a tax on Mehriehs that exceeded the standard rate—whether the sum of Mehrieh has been received by the woman or not; and 4) the insistence of the drafters on 13 as the age of marriage for women. Women's rights activists in the One Million Signatures Campaign hosted the first meeting to examine the Family Support Act, and issued a statement protesting the legislation. Other groups, including the Women's Commission of the Participation Front, the main reformist political party, held similar meetings. Following these activities, some female members of Parliament objected to certain provisions in the legislation as well. The legislation remains in the Parliamentary Commission, and has not yet been presented to the full Parliament for a vote. Women's rights activists have threatened to hold a demonstration in front of the Parliament should the Act come up for a vote.

Quotas to Limit Admittance of Female University Students to Centers of Higher Education. On 8 April 2008, a statement objecting to a governmental program designed to limit attendance and acceptance of female students in some fields of study within the higher education system was released. The statement was signed by over 700 student and women's rights activists. The program, which seeks to address and rectify the disproportionately high rate of university entrances by female students as compared to male students, secretly imposed limits on the acceptance of female students to certain fields of study. While this issue has been up for public debate for some time, no official legislation had been adopted to implement quotas on female students. But on 8 February 2008, the organization charged with the admission of university students to institutions of higher education (Sazeman Sanjesh) reluctantly admitted that they had been enforcing a quota system limiting the presence of female students in some fields of study for the academic years [20]06–07 and 07–08. The organization also admitted that they had been working to positively promote the acceptance of male university students into some fields of study with a formula of 30–40% female or male and 10% based on competition. The quota systems had been enforced in the academic year 06–07 for 26 fields and for 07–08 for 39 fields of study. It is worth mentioning that prior to being accepted to University, prospective students must take a rigorous and competitive entrance exam, and those scoring highest are accepted first. Women's rights and student rights activists have objected to this gender-based quota system, claiming that it limits women's participation in the social sphere, and in particular in an area where they have enjoyed great and justified success. Prior to the implementation of this quota system, the female acceptance rate to University was around 65%.

Closure of Zanan Monthly. On January 2008, the feminist monthly *Zanan* (Women) was banned by order of the Secretariat of the Press Oversight Council. The Council justified its decision by claiming *Zanan* to be "a radical feminist publication, engaged in publishing false claims of violence against women and unjustly criticizing laws governing the lives of women as discriminatory, exaggerating the negative conditions of women's lives, and damaging the image of the Basij Volunteer Force." The Council banned the monthly despite the fact that banning of publications is not one of its duties. *Zanan* is recognized as the first feminist publication in Iran. With a sixteen-year history, *Zanan* also boasts being the longest running feminist publication. Prior to its closure it provided the only print medium dedicated solely to addressing issues of importance to women, the concerns of women's rights activists, and developments in the women's movement. A supporter of the One Million Signatures Campaign, *Zanan* often covered news about developments within the Campaign, which most other print publications have refused to do. On the 13 February 2008, over 1500 persons objected to the closure of the monthly. *Zanan* is currently planning to object to the decision of the Council, and has lodged a court complaint asking for the reversal of the decision to ban the publication, on grounds that the action was illegal.

The Crackdown on Women's Rights Activists

As women's rights activists increased their demands for equal rights and voiced their opposition to policies that worked against women, the crackdown on women's rights activists including pressure by security agencies increased proportionately. . . .

Women's rights activists and their supporters called for a public protest in Tehran on 12 June 2006. During the days leading up to the planned demonstration, Judiciary officials summoned a number of these activists in an attempt to cancel the demonstration. On the evening of 10 June 2006, Judiciary agents delivered summonses to the homes of Parvin Ardalan, Sussan Tahmasebi, Noushin Ahmadi Khorasani, and Fariba Davoodi Mohajer. Ms. Shahla Entsari was arrested on the day of the protest at her place of employment and was held in detention for one day. She was later dismissed from her job. Ms. Davoodi Mohajer received her summons in person and turned herself in for interrogation on the day of the protest.

The demonstration was planned to take place in Haft Tir Square in central Tehran. When hundreds of demonstrators approached the Square on the afternoon of 12 June, they encountered a heavy presence of security forces and the police stationed around the square. The security forces prevented demonstrators from holding a peaceful assembly. They beat the demonstrators with batons, used pepper gas against them, and sprayed them with color paint to mark and arrest them.

Government forces detained a total of 70 men and women on that day. Over a period of one week, all of the detainees were released on bail except for Ali Akbar Mousavi Khoini, a former member of Parliament and human rights activist.

Khoini remained in detention for over four months, most of which was spent in solitary confinement. He received beatings and injuries during his time in detention. The authorities released him on bail on 22 October 2006. He was charged with acting against national security; the case remains open, with no court date scheduled. . . .

Keeping Opposition Groups in Check

Since its launch in August 2006, activists in the One Million Signatures Campaign have faced harassment and obstruction of their peaceful efforts by security forces. They have been systematically denied space for convening meetings. Additionally, activists have been arrested while collecting signatures in support of the Campaign's petition asking the Parliament to reform laws that discriminate against women, for convening meetings and for writing on the Campaign's website. To date [as of May 2008], 44 members of the Campaign have been arrested for alleged violations in relation to their peaceful activities in support of women's rights. . . .

Authorities have also systematically thwarted efforts by Campaign activists to convene meetings and gatherings in their homes. Since these activists have been denied permits to use public spaces for their meetings, they contend that they have no choice but to hold meetings in their homes. They further contend that convening meetings and gatherings in private homes is legal and does not endanger national security, as claimed by security and judiciary officials. According to Change for Equality, the website of the Campaign, the following individuals have been harassed for holding meetings and gatherings in their private homes, demonstrating the intent of security officials to obstruct and prevent their freedom of assembly: "In Tehran, the security police has summoned and interrogated Nafiseh Azad, Parastoo Allahyari, Najmeh Zare, Behnaz Shekaryar, Nasrin Farhoumand, and Khadijeh Moghadam for holding meetings at their private homes, or attending meetings of the Campaign. According to reports from the provinces, campaign members have also been interrogated in other cities, including in Isfahan, Shiraz, Kermanshah, Anzali, Rasht, and Hamedan."

> "The imposition of the autocratic rule of
> the shah on the people of Iran through
> the 1953 CIA [Central Intelligence
> Agency] coup ... postponed the ad-
> vancement of rights in Iran for de-
> cades."

U.S. Imperialism Has Impeded the Advancement of Women's Rights in Iran

Simin Royanian

*Simin Royanian asserts in the following viewpoint that the Is-
lamic revolution in Iran benefitted women's rights. Though not a
defender of the Islamic hard-line regime or its laws, Royanian
claims that the government set up after the revolution allowed
women to peaceably come together and work to change unjust or
unpopular rulings. She maintains that under the previous regime—run by the shah, who was a puppet of American interests—women did not have the freedom to form an opposition to
the state mandates. Thus, Royanian believes that U.S. imperialism has always impeded the growth of human rights by taking
the*

Simin Royanian, "Women's Rights in Iran," *Women for Peace and Justice in Iran*, March
25, 2005. Reproduced by permission.

side of restrictive governments that shut down avenues of protest. Royanian is a peace activist and cofounder of Women for Peace and Justice in Iran, *a Web site that examines human rights issues.*

As you read, consider the following questions:

1. What did women need to have in order to travel outside of Iran during the reign of the shah, as Royanian relates?

2. According to Royanian, what were some of the measures that the new Islamic government adopted to encourage the inclusion of women in the public sphere?

3. Why does the author compare women activists in Iran today to the American suffragettes who fought for the right to vote in the late-nineteenth and early-twentieth centuries?

R esponse to a question posted on Chicago indymedia:

. . .

[U]nder [the] shah [Mohammed Reza Pahlavi, 1941–1979] women had all the rights.

When Islam radicals took over they lost them.

How is that US imperialism?

Our response:

Women did not have all their rights under the Shah. Sharia Law was the law in Iran prior to 1979. The Islamic Sharia law was the basis of family, marriage and women's rights in Iran. As an example, the law permitted men to have four permanent and as many temporary wives as they wanted. Custody of children was in the hands of the father and after his death, in the hands of the male relatives on the father's side. So if the couple were divorced, even after the death of the father, the mother would not get custody.

The woman had to have written permission from her husband to travel. Since inside the country, one does not need to show an ID [identification] to travel, this permission was required for traveling outside the country. Citizenship was only through paternity. An Iranian man's child from any woman would become an Iranian citizen automatically. An Iranian woman's child from a non-Iranian would not be eligible for citizenship.

All these laws and many more were in place in Iran. Due to the rise of women's rights movements around the world, including Iran, certain advancements were being implemented gradually such as the right to vote, which was established in Iran in 1963.

One law (the "family protection law") that was passed in late 1970's required married men to get permission from their permanent wife, or wives, to acquire another permanent wife. This did not apply to temporary wives.

The Revolution Emphasized Inclusion

After the establishment of the Islamic government in Iran, a move was made to expand the Sharia law further. The outcome of the "fundamentalist" interpretation of Sharia in Iran, though not as harsh as in Saudi Arabia or that of the Taliban [in Afghanistan], did include the exclusion of women from judgeship, the imposition of Islamic code of dress on women, and inclusion of strict Sharia rules in the judiciary. These meant that some punishments for crimes were to comply with the Islamic tradition as interpreted by the ruling hard liners. It is important to realize that almost all countries with majority Moslem population follow some interpretation of Islamic law in their laws.

The new rulers, however, emphasized the early Islamic tradition of inclusion of women in civil and political life. The voting right for women was maintained and women were encouraged to participate fully in all forms public life. Conse-

Equitable Divorce Is a New Freedom

Women's rights advocates say Iranian women are displaying a growing determination to achieve equal status in this conservative Muslim theocracy, where male supremacy is still enscribed in the legal code. One in five marriages now end in divorce, according to government data, a fourfold increase in the past 15 years.

And it is not just women from the wealthy, Westernized elites. The family court building in Vanak Square here [in Tehran] is filled with women . . . who are not privileged. Women from lower classes and even the religious are among those marching up and down the stairs to fight for divorces and custody of their children.

Nazila Fathi,
"Starting at Home, Iran's Women Fight for Rights,"
New York Times, February 13, 2009.

quently a very complex and sophisticated system of inclusion and exclusion was developed. Meanwhile two types of women activism were developed. One was by the women who support an Islamic government but believe in a different interpretation than the hardliners, and the other by secular women. The secular women also practiced two forms of struggle. One was by women who published and worked in the legal interpretation of Sharia to promote a more liberal view. The other were the women who worked through long and difficult noncooperation, refusing to comply with the dress and behavior codes in social life, thus testing and pushing the limits.

As a result of the combination of all these efforts within and in opposition to the system women have made progress in many areas. Today [in 2005], female students form more than half of the entering class in Iran's universities. There are many more women in Parliament than there ever were during the previous government; there is a well developed birth control program in place which received an award from the UN [United Nations] about five years ago [in 1999].

According to UN WHO [World Health Organization] statistics, infant mortality and teen-age pregnancy rates in Iran are much lower than those in most third-world countries. For the last two years several women's organizations have publicly celebrated March 8th as International Women's Day in Tehran [Iran's capital] and other cities around the country. Now, there are women publishers and all-women publishing houses, printing books and pamphlets on women's issues from secular and even left points of view.

All of this in spite of, not because of the form of government in Iran.

Imperialism Always Impedes Human Rights Progress

This is true of all rights movements of people around the world. People have always struggled hard and long to gain their human rights. The suffragists in the US worked hard, went on hunger strikes and to prison, and it took them from 1848 (the first women's rights convention in Seneca Falls, New York) to 1920 to win the right to vote so they could participate in the political life of their country.

Colonialism and imperialism have always impeded the struggle of ordinary people to better their lives economically, socially, and politically. That is why the main impediment to the progress of human rights, including the rights of women is the intervention of US imperialism in the affairs of the people of the third world.

The imposition of the autocratic rule of the shah on the people of Iran through the 1953 CIA [Central Intelligence Agency] coup, the complete repression of any movement by the people, postponed the advancement of rights in Iran for decades. In addition, the elimination of any secular and left opposition to the rule of the Shah and US imperialism, contributed greatly to the superiority of the Islamic forces when the revolution was eventually won.

This is what Imperialism does. It supports the fundamentalist rule in Saudi Arabia, builds and arms the Taliban to overthrow a government friendly to the Soviet Union, arms and helps [Iraq's former leader] Saddam Hussein [fight a war] against the Iranian people for 8 years, supports the Turkish military massacre of the Kurdish people, assassinates democratically elected leaders in Latin America, and on and on. That is why US Imperialism has been and is the main impediment of peace and justice for people all over the world.

Periodical Bibliography

The following articles have been selected to supplement the diverse views presented in this chapter.

Timothy Garton Ash   "Let's Get Out of Their Way, at Least," *Globe & Mail* (Toronto, Canada), September 24, 2009.

Nazila Fathi   "Starting at Home, Iran's Women Fight for Rights," *New York Times*, February 13, 2009.

Akbar Ganji   "The Fight for Iran's Freedom," *Newsweek International*, February 18, 2008.

Noushin Ahmadi Khorasani   "Signed with an X," *New Internationalist*, March 2007.

Marek Lenarcik   "Women Campaign for Greater Rights as Iran Vote Nears," *Washington Times*, May 31, 2009.

Ramin Mostaghim and Jeffrey Fleishman   "Iranians Brace for Tougher Economic Times," *Los Angeles Times*, November 4, 2009.

Adel Safty   "Democracy Is Percolating in Iran," *Iran Times International*, July 10, 2009.

Charlie Savage and Mark Landler   "Black Market Shows Iran Can Adapt to Sanctions," *New York Times*, October 4, 2009.

Vivienne Walt   "How Badly Would Sanctions on Gas Imports Hurt Iran?" *Time*, September 30, 2009.

For Further Discussion

Chapter 1

1. Following the end of the Cold War, the international community embarked on a campaign of nuclear non-proliferation to stop the spread and development of nuclear weapons worldwide. Many countries have signed the nuclear non-proliferation treaty and pledged not to develop nuclear weapons. Even though Iran has signed the treaty, many political commentators contend that Iran is pursuing nuclear weapons and that their acquisition of these weapons would represent a unique threat to the United States and its allies. Conduct some outside research and determine whether you believe there is any reason for a state to develop nuclear weapons. Is there any benefit for a state owning nuclear weapons, as suggested by Michael C. Desch? Does a country's possession of a nuclear weapon only become a threat when it is a government unfriendly to the United States, as argued by Mortimer Zuckerman? Support your argument with quotes from the articles.

2. While both Matthew A. Levitt and Daniel Byman acknowledge that evidence exists to support a link between Iran and terrorist groups, the two differ in their assessment of whether Iran would provide terrorists with weapons of mass destruction. Levitt asserts that if Iran possessed nuclear capabilities, it would provide terrorist groups with nuclear weapons. Byman contends that the Iranian government would not pass nuclear weapons technology on to terrorists even though Iran has provided terrorists with financial, weapons, and ideological support in the past. Do you think it would benefit or harm Iran to

provide terrorists with nuclear weapons? Although there is evidence to show that Iran has supported terrorists in the past, do you believe that Iran would provide them with such destructive weapons technology? Why or why not? Use quotes from the authors to strengthen your claims.

3. Israel's relationship with the Arab and Muslim world is a flash point for controversy in the Middle East. Of all the countries in the region, many scholars and political commentators view Iran as one of the most significant threats to Israel's existence, and this view helps to shape American policy toward Iran. Reread the two viewpoints and determine whether you believe Iran does indeed present a threat to the existence of the Jewish state. Is the Iranian government really determined to destroy Israel as suggested by Michael Rubin? Or is the Iranian threat toward Israel exaggerated, as is argued by Jeremiah Haber? How should Israel's concerns impact American policy? Explain your answer.

Chapter 2

1. International relations among countries are often governed by diplomacy; however, under President George W. Bush, diplomatic relations between Iran and the United States were severed following Bush's speech in which he declared Iran to be part of the "Axis of Evil"—a triumvirate of rogue nations that included Iraq and North Korea. With the election of President Barack Obama in 2008, hopes were renewed that a meaningful relationship with Iran could be re-established to mitigate the threat Iranian possession of nuclear weapons poses. Reread the first two viewpoints in Chapter 2 and conduct some outside research into the current state of affairs between the United States and Iran. Has any progress been made in addressing the nuclear weapons issue? Are there signs that the rela-

tionship between the two countries will continue to improve in the future? Do you think diplomacy will be a successful mode for the United States to engage with Iran? Support your answer using current examples and quotes.

2. Economic sanctions often place limits on a country's imports and exports, thus crippling the economy and ultimately forcing the target of sanctions to give in to external demands. U.S. sanctions on Iran are designed to bring about regime change or compel the current government to become more open and responsive to the international community. James Phillips believes that U.S. sanctions have not been severe enough to achieve these goals. Djavad Salehi-Isfahani contends that there is no evidence that sanctions thus far have produced any meaningful change in the Iranian government's behavior and should not be continued as a foreign policy tool. Do you agree with Phillips' or Salehi-Isfahani's view? What effect do you think sanctions have had on Iran?

3. John R. Bolton believes that intimidation and diplomacy have failed to bring down the oppressive regime in Iran. He therefore contends that reaching out to young Iranians and supporting an overthrow of the government is the best course for U.S. policy. Ted Galen Carpenter and Jessica Ashooh warn that any intrusion on the part of the United States is likely to be detrimental to any anti-government movement because Iranians recall that the last time Washington was involved in Iranian regime change it ousted a popular president and reinstated the unpopular rule of the shah. How do you think the United States could effectively support a grassroots revolution in Iran without seeming to orchestrate it purely for America's benefit? Use the articles to support your conclusions.

Chapter 3

1. Do some research on Iranian presidential candidate Mir Hossein Mousavi, then address Mehdi Khalaji's claim that Mousavi might not be the true revolutionary that Iran needs. Do you think Mousavi's platform is sufficiently radical to bring about meaningful change in Iran? Explain your answer using quotes from the articles in this chapter and any outside readings you have gathered.

2. Do you believe there is any evidence that the current Iranian regime is likely to loosen its grip on the populace or even collapse in the face of popular protest? What hopeful signs do the authors of this chapter concede? What conclusions do they draw that would suggest the regime will outlast the protests? Look at other news sources to inform yourself on the most recent signs of resentment and resistance before finalizing your response.

3. After reviewing the final pair of articles in this chapter and any outside reading you deem useful, rate President Barack Obama's response to the anti-government demonstrations in Iran. How effective has he been in showing U.S. support for the protesters? What opportunities might he have missed by sticking to his policy?

Chapter 4

1. Patrick Clawson argues that Iran's government has failed to diversify its markets and relies too much on oil profits to create a stable economy. William R. Hawkins asserts that it is the lack of foreign investment—scared off by U.S. sanctions—that has kept Iran from expanding its petroleum production to fuel greater economic growth overall. After reading both arguments, decide what you think is the stronger tether on Iran's economy. What do you think Iran needs to do to bring about greater prosperity? Explain your answer with quotes from the viewpoints.

2. Simin Royanian is one of many Iranian women's advocates who refute the accusation that women in Iran are helpless victims of a misogynistic regime. What kinds of rights do women enjoy in post-revolution Iran? What restrictions on women's rights are women fighting to overcome? Examine other testimony from Iranian women to help flesh out your responses.

Organizations to Contact

The editors have compiled the following list of organizations concerned with the issues debated in this book. The descriptions are derived from materials provided by the organizations. All have publications or information available for interested readers. The list was compiled on the date of publication of the present volume; the information provided here may change. Be aware that many organizations take several weeks or longer to respond to inquiries, so allow as much time as possible.

American Enterprise Institute for Public Policy Research (AEI)

1150 17th St. NW, Washington, DC 20036
(202) 862-5800 • fax: (202) 862-7177
Web site: www.aei.org

A conservative public policy organization, AEI promotes the ideas of limited government, private enterprise, individual liberty, and vigilant national defense and foreign policies. Publications written by the institute's scholars in combination with national conferences form the basis of the organization's analysis of current issues in U.S. government policy. Numerous AEI reports and conferences have addressed the potential outcomes of American intervention in Iran and have debated the appropriate support the United States should provide to Israel in the event that it sees an attack on Iran necessary for its own safety and survival. *The American* is the bimonthly magazine of AEI; the AEI Web site provides articles from this publication as well as other publications and commentary.

American Israel Public Affairs Committee (AIPAC)

251 H St. NW, Washington, DC 20001
(202) 639-5200 • fax: (202) 347-4918
Web site: www.aipac.org

AIPAC lobbies the American government to take steps to ensure Israel's security through a strong, pro-Israel U.S. foreign policy. The committee contends that an Israeli-American alliance is necessary to establish stability in the Middle East. AIPAC supports an increase in crippling sanctions on Iran to influence the Islamic Republic's pursuit of nuclear weapons. Reports discussing Iran such as "The Iranian Nuclear Threat," "Iran's Support for Terrorism," and "Iranian Defiance Demands Crippling Sanctions" can all be read on the AIPAC Web site.

Brookings Institution

1775 Massachusetts Ave. NW, Washington, DC   20036
(202) 797-6000
e-mail: communications@brookings.edu
Web site: www.brookings.edu

The Brookings Institution provides independent research about current public policy issues in an attempt to formulate government policy that improves life for Americans and both opens and strengthens the international system. The institution views Iran as a continuing force of instability on the international scene due to its attempts to develop nuclear weapons, its support for insurgents in Iraq, and its ties to terrorist groups such as Hamas and Hezbollah. Brookings Institution scholars examine both past and present actions of Iran in reports, including "The Iran Hostage Crisis: 30 Years Later," "Iran and Mahmoud Ahmadinejad's Second Term," and "Political and Economic Woes Thwart Return to Normalcy in Iran."

Carnegie Endowment for International Peace

1779 Massachusetts Ave. NW, Washington, DC   20036-2103
(202) 483-7600 • fax: (202) 483-1840
e-mail: info@carnegieendowment.org
Web site: www.carnegieendowment.org

The Carnegie Endowment has been working for nearly a century to increase cooperation among all nations and to advance the United States' role as an leader that promotes global peace and stability. Thus, Iran's actions as well as the United States' reactions to these behaviors are of central concern to the organization's scholars. Publications such as "Engagement with Iran: An Assessment of Options" and "Reading Khamenei: The World View of Iran's Most Powerful Leader," assess the conditions in Iran and the options for U.S. involvement. These reports and others can be read on the organization's Web site.

Cato Institute

1000 Massachusetts Ave. NW, Washington, DC   20001-5403
(202) 842-0200 • fax: (202) 842-3490
Web site: www.cato.org

The Cato Institute works to promote the libertarian ideas of free market economics and limited government intervention in both the social and economic lives of Americans, while rejecting overzealous military intervention in foreign affairs. Institute scholars have analyzed the options for U.S. involvement in Iran in reports such as "The Bottom Line on Iran: The Costs and Benefits of Preventative War versus Deterrence." Daily podcasts, including "Known Unknowns, Iran and Nukes" and "How Things Can Get Worse in Iran," provide current assessments of the situation in that country. Cato's numerous publications include the tri-annual *Cato Journal*, the quarterly *Cato's Letters*, and the quarterly *Regulation*.

Center for Strategic and International Studies (CSIS)

1800 K St. NW, Washington, DC   20006
(202) 887-0200 • fax: (202) 775-3199
Web site: www.csis.org

CSIS is a public policy organization dedicated to providing timely, bipartisan policy advice concerning current global issues based on extensive research and debate. The organization's Middle East Program contains its work on Iran, which focuses mainly on Iran's development of nuclear weapons. Publications include "Iran's Nuclear Negotiations and the West" and "Iran Status Report: Iran and the Challenges to U.S. Policy." The *Washington Quarterly* is the official publication of CSIS.

Council on Foreign Relations (CFR)

The Harold Pratt House, 58 E 68th St., New York, NY 10065

(212) 434-9400 • fax: (212) 434-9800

Web site: www.cfr.org

CFR is a nonpartisan membership organization that seeks to foster an increased understanding of foreign policy concerns through its sponsorship of meetings for global leaders to debate current issues, its operation of a think tank where scholars from a variety of backgrounds can provide current commentary on foreign policy, and its publication of books and reports. CFR's background reports do not take a specific stance on any issue but provide extensive information about a range of topics. CFR's coverage of Iran focuses on the country's acquisition of nuclear technology, the possibility of an Israeli offensive strike, and international cooperation to influence the Iranian regime. CFR publishes the bimonthly magazine *Foreign Affairs*.

Foundation for Democracy in Iran (FDI)

11140 Rockville Pike, Suite 100, Rockville, MD 20852

(301) 946-2918 • fax: (301) 942-5341

e-mail: exec@iran.org

Web site: www.iran.org

FDI was founded in 1995 to help promote democracy and human rights in Iran. Throughout Iran's 2009 elections, the organization's site posted updates concerning the protests in Iran that erupted in response to the reelection of President Mahmoud Ahmadinejad. The FDI Web site provides current information about ongoing efforts by Iranians to oppose their government.

Heritage Foundation

214 Massachusetts Ave. NE, Washington, DC 20002-4999

(202) 546-4400 • fax: (202) 546-8328

e-mail: info@heritage.org

Web site: www.heritage.org

A conservative think tank, the Heritage Foundation works to preserve the principles of limited government, free market economics, and a strong national defense in America. The Heritage Foundation warns that the Tehran government of Mahmoud Ahmadinejad represents a growing threat to regional and international stability and security due to Iran's longstanding support of terrorism and its more recent attempts to construct nuclear weapons. Reports and commentary discussing the situation in Iran and possible American responses, including "Bomb or Surrender: Not America's Only Options Regarding Iran," "All a Twitter: How Social Networking Shaped Iran's Election Protests," and "Obama Administration Must Speak Out Against Iran's Clenched Fist," can be accessed via the Internet.

Hoover Institution on War, Revolution, and Peace

434 Galvez Mall, Stanford University
Stanford, CA   94305-6010
(650) 723-1754 • fax: (650) 723-1687
Web site: www.hoover.org

The Hoover Institution conducts comprehensive analysis of politics, economics, and international affairs. Scholars at the institution compose and publish research and commentary on a wide variety of topics in an effort to further the debate on current issues, both national and global. The Iran Democracy Project (IDP) is one attempt by the organization to delve deeper into the issues surrounding a current topic of interest. The IDP was formed to increase Western understanding of the prospects for democracy in the Middle East by focusing first on democracy in Iran; findings by the project can be found on the IDP Web site. The Hoover Institution's bimonthly publication *Policy Review* and the quarterly *Hoover Digest* provide additional information about Iran and U.S. interests there.

International Campaign for Human Rights in Iran

(917) 669-5996
e-mail: hadighaemi@iranhumanrights.org
Web site: www.iranhumanrights.org

The International Campaign for Human Rights in Iran was founded to direct attention to the human rights abuses committed in Iran and to drive the international community to action to prevent further abuses. The campaign provides detailed information about individuals imprisoned in Iran, limits to academic freedom, and the denial of workers' and women's rights. Specific information about these topics can be found on the campaign's Web site. Copies of publications such as "Report on the Status of Women Human Rights Defenders: April 2009," "Workers' Rights," and "The Systematic Repression of the Women's Rights Movement: 2008" can be obtained online.

Middle East Forum (MEF)
1500 Walnut St., Suite 1050, Philadelphia, PA   19102
(215) 546-5406 • fax: (215) 546-5409
e-mail: info@meforum.org
Web site: www.meforum.org

The MEF sees the Middle East as a continuing problem for the United States and its allies due to the abundance of dictatorships, radical ideologies and extremism, violence, terrorism, and conflict in the region. As a public policy think tank, the forum works to define America's role in the region and to protect U.S. interests and allies. The forum believes that Iran is a threat to the United States and its allies and therefore must be contained and denied nuclear weapons capabilities. MEF's official publication, *Middle East Quarterly*, provides in-depth research and articles concerning Iran.

Middle East Institute (MEI)
1761 N St. NW, Washington, DC   20036-2882
(202) 785-1141 • fax: (202) 331-8861
Web site: www.mei.edu

MEI has been working since 1946 to establish an improved relationship and understanding between Americans and people from the Middle East. MEI seeks to achieve this goal through its publications and educational lectures and conferences.

Publications discussing Iran specifically include "The Scorpion's Sting and the Python's Grip," "What Threat Does Iran Really Pose to Israel?" and "Iran and the U.S.: Time to Move On." These articles and others can be accessed on MEI's Web site.

Middle East Policy Council (MEPC)

1730 M St. NW, Suite 512, Washington, DC   20036
(202) 296-6767
e-mail: info@mepc.org
Web site: www.mepc.org

Since 1981, MEPC has offered political analysis of issues in the Middle East and has fostered debate and education by hosting conferences for educators and government officials. The searchable archives of the council's quarterly journal *Middle East Policy* contain numerous articles discussing the current situation in Iran as well as options for U.S. engagement with the country. Lists of additional resources also are provided on the MEPC Web site.

Project on Middle East Democracy (POMED)

1820 Jefferson Pl. NW, Washington, DC   20036
(202) 828-9660
Web site: www.pomed.org

POMED seeks to analyze the ways in which democratic reform in the Middle East could benefit the region and its people and to make suggestions as to how the United States could further this process. The organization uses dialogue, research, and advocacy to advance these goals. In the wake of the 2009 elections in Iran, POMED has carefully followed developments and assessed the situation as it continues to change within the country. The POMED Web site provides articles and reports by project scholars concerning democracy in Iran and other Middle Eastern countries.

Washington Institute for Near East Policy

1828 L St. NW, Suite 1050, Washington, DC   20036

(202) 452-0650 • fax: (202) 223-5364
Web site: www.washingtoninstitute.org

The Washington Institute for Near East Policy works to provide a more nuanced understanding of the relationship between the United States and the Middle East at large. Additionally, the organization asserts that peace and stability in the
region can be achieved only if all parties remain actively engaged. Institute research on Iran focuses on the country's support of terrorism, the dangers of their acquisition of nuclear
weapons, and the impact that foreign economic pressure could
exert on the governing regime. Reports on these issues and
others are all available on the institute's Web site.

Bibliography of Books

Ervand
Abrahamian

A History of Modern Iran. New York:
Cambridge University Press, 2008.

Arshin
Adib-Moghaddam

*Iran in World Politics: The Question of
the Islamic Republic.* New York:
Columbia University Press, 2008.

Ali M. Ansari

*Confronting Iran: The Failure of
American Foreign Policy and the Next
Great Crisis in the Middle East.* New
York: Basic, 2006.

Ali M. Ansari

*Iran Under Ahmadinejad: The Politics
of Confrontation.* New York:
Routledge, 2007.

Michael Axworthy

*A History of Iran: Empire of the
Mind.* New York: Basic, 2008.

Fakhreddin Azimi

*The Quest for Democracy in Iran: A
Century of Struggle Against
Authoritarian Rule.* Cambridge, MA:
Harvard University Press, 2008.

Daniel Byman

*Deadly Connections: States That
Sponsor Terrorism.* New York:
Cambridge University Press, 2005.

Hamid Dabashi

Iran: A People Interrupted. New York:
New Press, 2007.

James Dobbins

*Coping with Iran: Confrontation,
Containment, or Engagement?: A
Conference Report.* Santa Monica, CA:
RAND, 2007.

Anoushiravan Ehteshami

After Khomeini. New York: Routledge, 1995.

Anoushiravan Ehteshami and Mahjoob Zweiri

Iran and the Rise of Its Neoconservatives: The Politics of Tehran's Silent Revolution. New York: I.B. Tauris, 2007.

Behrooz Ghamari-Tabrizi

Islam and Dissent in Post-Revolutionary Iran: Abdolkarim Soroush, Religious Politics, and Democratic Reform. New York: I.B. Tauris, 2008.

Ali Gheissari, ed.

Contemporary Iran: Economy, Society, Politics. New York: Oxford University Press, 2009.

Nathan Gonzalez

Engaging Iran: The Rise of a Middle East Powerhouse and America's Strategic Choice. Westport, CT: Praeger, 2007.

Jerrold D. Green, Frederic Wehrey, and Charles Wolf Jr.

Understanding Iran. Santa Monica, CA: RAND, 2009.

Judith Palmer Harik

Hezbollah: The Changing Face of Terrorism. New York: I.B. Tauris, 2004.

Milton M. Hoenig

The New Iranian Leadership. Westport, CT: Praeger, 2008.

Mehri Honarbin-Holliday

Becoming Visible in Iran: Women in Contemporary Iranian Society. New York: Tauris Academic Studies, 2008.

Roger Howard   *Iran Oil: The New Middle East Challenge to America.* New York: I.B. Tauris, 2007.

Alireza Jafarzadeh   *The Iran Threat: President Ahmadinejad and the Coming Nuclear Crisis.* New York: Palgrave, 2007.

Michael Ledeen   *The Iranian Time Bomb: The Mullah Zealots' Quest for Destruction.* New York: St. Martin's, 2007.

John W. Limbert   *Negotiating with Iran: Wrestling the Ghosts of History.* Washington, DC: U.S. Institute of Peace Press, 2009.

Alidad Mafinezam   *Iran and Its Place Among Nations.*
and Aria Mehrabi   Westport, CT: Praeger, 2008.

Hooman Majd   *The Ayatollah Begs to Differ: The Paradox of Modern Iran.* New York: Doubleday, 2008.

Arzoo Osanloo   *The Politics of Women's Rights in Iran.* Princeton, NJ: Princeton University Press, 2009.

Meghen   *Shrewd Sanctions: Statecraft and State*
O'Sullivan   *Sponsors of Terrorism.* Washington, DC: Brookings Institution, 2003.

Trita Parsi   *Treacherous Alliance: The Secret Dealings of Israel, Iran, and the U.S.* New Haven, CT: Yale University Press, 2007.

Kenneth Pollack   *The Persian Puzzle.* New York: Random House, 2004.

Scott Ritter — *Target Iran: The Truth About the White House's Plans for Regime Change.* New York: Nation Books, 2006.

Hamideh Sedghi — *Women and Politics in Iran: Veiling, Unveiling, and Reveiling.* New York: Cambridge University Press, 2007.

Ghoncheh Tazmini — *Khatami's Iran: The Islamic Republic and the Turbulent Path to Reform.* New York: Tauris Academic Studies, 2009.

Index